W9-CFV-849

DISSERTATION PROPOSAL GUIDEBOOK

DISSERTATION PROPOSAL GUIDEBOOK

How to Prepare a Research Proposal and Get It Accepted

By

DAVID C. GARDNER

and

GRACE JOELY BEATTY

CHARLES C THOMAS · PUBLISHER

Springfield · Illinois · U.S.A.

Published and Distributed Throughout the World by

CHARLES C THOMAS ● PUBLISHER

Bannerstone House

301-327 East Lawrence Avenue, Springfield, Illinois, U.S.A.

This book is protected by copyright. No part of it
may be reproduced in any manner without
written permission from the publisher.

© *1980, by* CHARLES C THOMAS ● PUBLISHER

ISBN 0-398-04086-9 (cloth)

ISBN 0-398-04087-7 (paper)

Library of Congress Catalog Card Number: 80-12719

With THOMAS BOOKS *careful attention is given to all details of
manufacturing and design. It is the Publisher's desire to present books that
are satisfactory as to their physical qualities and artistic possibilities and
appropriate for their particular use.* THOMAS BOOKS *will be true to those
laws of quality that assure a good name and good will.*

Printed in the United States of America
V-R-1

Library of Congress Cataloging in Publication Data

Gardner, David C
    Dissertation proposal guidebook.

    Bibliography: p.
    Includes index.
    1. Dissertations, Academic--Handbooks, manuals, etc.
I. Beatty, Grace Joely, joint author. II. Title.
LB2369.G26   808'.02   80-12719
ISBN 0-398-04086-9
ISBN 0-398-04087-7 (pbk.)

BIOGRAPHICAL SKETCHES

DR. DAVID C. GARDNER has both international and national professional work experience in education and industry spanning a twenty year period. Currently, he is an Associate Professor of Special and Counselor Education, Boston University. A prolific author and research design specialist, Doctor Gardner has many years of experience as a journal editor and dissertation advisor.

He served as the Principal Investigator and Director of several large Federally-funded projects on curriculum modification for handicapped students in vocational training programs 1975-1979. He is a member of the Board of Directors, National Association for Career Education (past president) and a founding officer and former Board Member of the Eastern Educational Research Association. Doctor Gardner is a member of the National Ethics Committee of the American Association on Mental Deficiency and was recently nominated for a Division Vice Presidency. He is a member of the Research Committee, Division on Career Development, Council for Exceptional Children. He recently received the Professional Award, American Association on Mental Deficiency, Region X and was selected for *Who's Who in Education* (1979).

DR. GRACE JOELY BEATTY is currently Managing Director of American Training and Research Associates, Inc. Doctor Beatty has national work experience in both education and industry covering an eleven year period of rapid professional growth. She has served as the Director of a major Federally-funded project at Boston University and held Senior Research Associate and Visiting Lecturer appointments at the University for several years. The author of numerous publications and a data analysis specialist, she has extensive experience in working individually with doctoral students.

She is a member of the Board of Directors of American Training and Research Associates, Inc., and has held a number of offices in national and regional professional organizations. Doctor Beatty was elected an "Outstanding Young Woman of America" in 1978.

PREFACE

THE need for a guidebook on dissertation proposal writing became evident while the authors planned for and conducted workshops on proposal writing through a program sponsored by American Training and Research Associates, Inc. of Methuen, Massachusetts. The training manual developed for these workshops is currently being used in research seminars at Boston University. Based on comments from our students, the training manual evolved into this guidebook.

This is not a complete work on how to write a dissertation, nor is it intended to be one. The scope of such a work would indeed be formidable! Rather, this work is a *guidebook*, a collection of models to be used by the graduate student who is developing his/her first major work — the dissertation or thesis. This is *not* a book on design or statistics, and it assumes that the student has had some coursework in those areas. It is quite literally a "cookbook" full of examples and tips. We expect that this first edition will be altered many times over the coming years as we receive feedback from our readers and students.

D.C.G.
G.J.B.

ACKNOWLEDGMENTS

WE wish to acknowledge the long-term support of our colleagues, Louis P. Aikman and Sue Allen Warren, of Boston University. We want to thank Dean Boyd E. Dewey, Jr. for his reading of the manuscript, his helpful comments, and his enthusiastic support of this project. We want to express our gratitude to Paula L. Gardner, Boston University, for her many suggestions, for her reading of the manuscript, and for her "fine tuning."

Lastly, we acknowledge gratefully the students who took the time to make helpful suggestions on the early version of the guidebook as well as the following colleagues who gave us permission to cite liberally from their dissertations and dissertation proposals:

Dr. John A. Curry, Senior Vice President
Northeastern University
Boston, Massachusetts

Dr. Boyd E. Dewey, Jr., Assistant Dean
Boston University
School of Education
Boston, Massachusetts

Dr. Betty Jane Grossman, Guidance Counselor
Newton Public Schools
Newton, Massachusetts

Dr. Margaret A. Kurtz, Professor and Chairperson
Department of Business
Colby-Sawyer College
New London, New Hampshire

D.C.G.
G.J.B.

CONTENTS

SECTION I
ORGANIZING THE DISSERTATION

Chapter

SECTION II
MODELS

DISSERTATION
PROPOSAL
GUIDEBOOK

Section I

Organizing the Dissertation

> *There is no substitute for hard work and perseverance.*

This section is designed to get you started. Your first goal is to *organize yourself* so that you can begin writing your dissertation proposal.

Chapter 1

GETTING YOUR ACT TOGETHER

SOME COMMON PROBLEMS

Laziness

"**I** WORKED hard at school/college/job today. I'm really beat. I'll wait until tomorrow. Besides, it is Monday Night Football/Tuesday Night at the Movies/Time Magazine night, etc."

Writing is an incredibly difficult and absorbing job. It requires self discipline. Find a place and a time where you can work. For some people, a rented room in a motel for two weeks does the trick. For others, regularly scheduled hours four mornings a week from 4 AM to 8 AM is sufficient. We all have our needs and methods, but the methods should include daily, weekly, and monthly goals. (For those of you who have short attention spans, try hourly goals.) You must choose the method that is best for *you*. Try anything; but for heaven's sake, work. If you don't work at it, you will never get the job done!

Money

Money is one of the most common excuses for not doing the dissertation given by the graduate school dropout. "But I have to feed my family. I have to work." Nonsense, *all* of us who have finished had problems. The vision of starving children just won't work. The senior author lived in a slum. His endodontist lived in a cold-water basement apartment in Montreal. The junior author went into debt for thousands of dollars. The senior author has had a doctoral student who managed to complete the residency with eight children, another who managed to run a large university in his spare time, etc. The lack of money excuse is worthless. If you want to finish, you will "delay gratification for larger future rewards." (Note: this

5

phrase is often used as a definition of maturity.)

Pride a.k.a. Insecurity

."I'm a school superintendent (or a principal, psychologist, manager, etc.) What can this professor teach me?"

"This is outmoded tradition. What is it going to prove? I'm already there as a professional."

Believe us, there is *no one* who does a quality dissertation who does not learn and grow from the experience. You'll just have to take our word for this until you join the club of those who have undergone their baptism by fire. In the meantime, ask yourself if you are "too good" to do it or whether the real reason you keep coming up with excuses is because you are, in fact, afraid. To misquote: "There is nothing to fear in the dissertation writing process but your own insecurities."

Stubbornness

Don't get so hung up on a topic that you refuse to change. Don't be determined to solve the problems of the world with your dissertation. Don't insist on answering the one burning question in your field and in the process make yourself famous and/or rich.

The dissertation is the *beginning* of your research career not the culmination. If you are able to complete a quality dissertation in as short a time as possible, you will have the rest of your life to solve the problems of the world — and get paid to do it. If your advisor doesn't like the topic or considers the scope too global, be willing to consider a change or prepare yourself for an uphill battle. The choice is yours.

Despair

Murphy's Law inevitably affects us all. No kidding. If something can go wrong, even with the most carefully planned project, it will. That is the pain and the joy of work in our field. If you let it get you down, you will find yourself literally up to your hindquarters in hopelessness. Fortunately, there is a cure for hopelessness. It is called *hard work* seasoned with the following:

1. Self-discipline.
2. Goal-directedness.
3. Acceptance of personal responsibility for the work.
4. A sense of humor.
5. Self-confidence.

So stop making excuses: stop blaming your job, your advisor, your wife/husband/kids/mother/dad/dogs/lack of income . . . (you fill in the rest). There is only one, and we repeat *only one*, person responsible for your dissertation — you. If you don't make it, it's your fault. You did not apply yourself. Let's face it, if you are an admitted candidate in a reputable graduate school, the faculty have already decided that you are capable. Otherwise, you would not have been admitted, or the school is disreputable. You must make the decision to work hard and persevere.

In our estimation, the difference between many of those who complete a graduate program and those who do not is related to whether or not they were required to write a detailed and concise plan for their research work before commencing: "Since good research must be carefully planned and systematically carried out, procedures that are improvised from step to step will not suffice. A worthwhile research project is likely to result only from a well-designed proposal" (Best, 1970, p. 26).

It is the philosophy of the authors that the well-designed proposal is the most efficient and effective way, in fact the *only* way, to complete a dissertation in the social sciences. In fact, our philosophy is that the proposal should be the dissertation written in the future tense and missing only the "Results and Discussion" section. Thus, this guidebook assumes that you, the reader, are now ready to write your dissertation even though you may not have chosen your topic. Are you ready?

Before you read the rest of this guidebook, sit down and make a list of as many excuses for not working on the dissertation as you can. Study them carefully, then throw the list in the wastebasket. You are now ready to roll up your sleeves and go to work.

Chapter 2

CHOOSING A TOPIC

THE most difficult task in getting a dissertation proposal together is usually choosing a topic. The following are some common mistakes in choosing a problem (paraphrased from Isaac, 1977, p. 2):

1. Collecting a lot of information with no particular plan or purpose and then figuring "I'll make some sense out of this later." If your advisor is letting you do this, he/she needs help too.
2. Taking a bunch of data that is already available in your school or workplace (or a friend's data) and trying to fit some meaningful research question to it.
3. Defining your operational terms, objectives, questions, in such an ambiguous or general way that your deductions, conclusions, etc., are probably invalid and useless.
4. Doing *ad hoc* research that is unique to a specific situation or environment and which will make no contribution to anything, much less to the literature.
5. Not basing research on a theoretical/empirical base. *The key to a quality dissertation is to use a sound theoretical/empirical base for hypothesis development.*
6. Not making clear your project's assumptions or limitations.
7. Failure to anticipate rival hypotheses (other possible explanations) for the outcomes of your study.

A Recipe for Picking a Topic

Step 1: Pick a Population

Many researchers will give you a different ("pure") approach. The reality of the situation is that you need to have a place to do your study and most of us can't spend thousands of dollars or thousands of hours on a dissertation. The main thing is to have a population with easy access and one over which you have a degree of control. We've seen lots of dissertations fail because the investigator couldn't get adequate collaboration or control of the treatment.

Step 2: Interest

Now that you have a population, answer the question "What can I study about the subjects that is of interest to me?" If you really don't have an interest, what is your advisor's interest? Go read what he/she has written. *If your advisor is not publishing, get another advisor.* The best dissertation advisor is one who keeps on doing research and writing after his/her dissertation. (There are exceptions of course. Some excellent teachers of research methods can't find the time required to write because they spend all their time rescuing doctoral students.)

It is usually helpful to pick a topic within the area of your advisor's expertise. First, he or she will want to help you more, and, secondly, he or she will be able to give you a lot more help since they are usually up on the literature in that particular field. (Quote your advisor and other committee members often.)

Step 3: The Library

Do not let the size of the library overpower you. Our recommendation is to spend a minimum amount of time in the library at first. This is a common cop-out: "I've spent *weeks* in the library reading."

That is *not* the way to find a topic. Instead, spend an afternoon browsing through *current* issues of journals in your field of interest. Literally hundreds of possible topics will materialize before your very eyes! Get a couple of recent articles on the area of your choice, and use their bibliographies as a starting point. Get copies of those references mentioned in the article that seem most relevant to your interest area. Use the bibliographies of those articles to refer you to more articles, etc.

Conduct a computer search. This will help you narrow your interest area and also saves time. If you don't know about computer searches, ask your librarian. Also, ask your librarian for advice on where to get information about your interest area.

This can save you hours.

Once you have found a specific area, you will need to get informal approval and suggestions from your advisor before completing your literature review. Remember, the purpose of the review is to find out if someone else has done the study and what studies can help you in refining your problem and in designing your study.

Step 4: Instrumentation

Select your instruments early in the game. This way you don't have to spend a lot of time defining your dependent variable(s). They will be defined by your measures. For instance, if your study is concerned with the effects of drinking Coca Cola® on career maturity, you might use Crites Career Maturity Inventory, Attitude Scale as your measure. Thus career maturity is defined by the Crites instrument.

Step 5: Treatment

You need to determine a treatment that will have some effect on your dependent variable and answer your research question. If we want to know what effects Coca Cola has on career maturity, it is obvious that the population will be scheduled to drink Coke on a predetermined schedule. The next question is *will* they drink it? You get the idea. . . .

Remember, you cannot go beyond Step 3 without having a very specific problem. The basic difficulty is in making up your own mind on which question to answer. Don't try to solve the problems of the world. Try only to demonstrate to your committee, and more importantly to yourself, that you know how to plan, organize, implement, and conduct good research and that you know how to finish the job with a high degree of proficiency. Try to pick a problem that is based in previous research, related to a theory, and can be studied efficiently and effectively. Longitudinal studies are for institutes that are funded over a long period of time or for students who are independently wealthy.

Let us give you an example of how a problem can be found

relatively easily:

Go to current issues of the most prestigious research journal in your field. Read articles in your area of interest, and look for an article where the author mentions in conclusion "that there is a great need for future research" in a specific area. In fact, the author says that there have been few studies concerned with this problem. Go read the *few* studies that the author cites on this problem and answer the following questions:

yes___ no___ Can you answer the question in a different way with your available population?

yes___ no___ Can you convince your advisor to buy this topic?

yes___ no___ Is it related to a sound theory?

yes___ no___ Can the study be accomplished in a reasonable length of time and at reasonable cost?

yes___ no___ Do you have the know-how and skills to implement such a study (or can you acquire them quickly)?

yes___ no___ Do you like this topic?

If the answer to all these questions is yes, you now have the perfect topic.

Chapter 3

GETTING DOWN TO THE NITTY GRITTY

N OW that you have decided on your topic and your problem, at least to the point where you can say "I'm planning to study the effects of X on Y," the next question is where do you begin writing. The answer is that you must try to draft a number of key sections *all at once.* These key elements of the dissertation must follow logically from one to the other, which means that as changes are made in one section, corresponding changes must be made in each of the other sections. The writing process looks something like the following:

KEY ELEMENTS IN WRITING

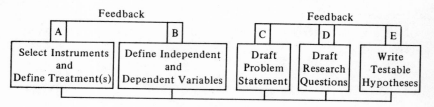

FEEDBACK

Example of A and B (Rough Draft)

DEFINE TREATMENT(S).
1. Goal-setting procedure on a work performance task in which the supervisor sets the employee's goal (Treatment$_1$).
2. Goal-setting procedure on a work performance task in which the employee sets own goals (Treatment$_2$).
3. No goal setting by employees on work performance task (No Treatment).

DEFINE INDEPENDENT VARIABLES. Defined here as the method of goal setting: (1) self-set; (2) supervisor set; (3) no goal setting.
    SELECT INSTRUMENTS. In the case of this production task

12

(making widgets), instrumentation consists of a Production Record Sheet, designed to record the number of widgets produced per shift by each employee. If you are trying to affect something that is less concrete than production scores, such as career maturity, self-concept, anxiety level, etc., you will need to select a test or instrument that has tested reliability and validity.

DEFINE DEPENDENT VARIABLE(S). The dependent variable is defined as the average number of widgets completed per shift. (Since you are dealing with a treatment applied to *groups* of people, then you must measure what happens to the *group* score — the average or mean score).

The next step is to get a good draft of your problem statement done and follow this with a statement of research questions and the hypotheses deduced from the problem statement/research questions. This cluster of key elements must fit logically together with the definition of the independent/dependent variable(s) previously drafted.

Example of C, D, and E

DRAFT PROBLEM STATEMENT. This study will investigate the effects of goal-setting procedures on the work performance of assembly-line employees. The investigation will be conducted in a "real work" setting and will use a "real work task" for which the trainee employees will be paid. The present study, within the context of a work training environment, will be concerned with the following research questions:

1. Does the procedure of goal setting, consisting of giving the trainee information on previous performance and then setting a goal for performance on the next task, increase the performance of the employee as compared to employees not setting goals?
2. Does the method of goal setting — having the shop supervisor set individual goals for each employee versus having each employee set his own goals — affect task performance?

HYPOTHESIS 1. (See research question No. 1 and compare.)

The mean production per shift of the combined groups of goal-setting employees will be significantly greater than the mean production of the no-goal setting group of employees. (This is a research, or directional, hypothesis.)

HYPOTHESIS 2. (See research question No. 2 and compare.)

There will be no significant differences in the mean production per shift of the employees in the two goal-setting groups. (This is what is known as a null hypothesis.)

The use of directional hypotheses versus null hypotheses depends upon your advisor. Some researchers prefer all hypotheses to be stated in the null. The authors believe that if you have theoretical and empirical support for a directional hypothesis then you should state it that way.

Hypothesis 1 was stated as a research hypothesis (directional) because there is theoretical and empirical support for the proposition that goal setting increases performance. Hypothesis 2 was stated in the null because of lack of theoretical and empirical support that different types of goal-setting procedures produce differing performance rates.

Note that in writing the two hypotheses we have begun to talk in statistical terms. The words *mean* and *significant* are statistical terminology. We have also specified that we are comparing *three* groups for *differences* and have specified the method of quantification as the average number of widgets (instrumentation.) In other words, this procedure roughs out the key elements of your dissertation, including the methodology section.

Key Methodology Elements

1. *Population*: Already selected. In our example, employees who are trainees in assembling widgets.
2. *Treatments*: Already roughed out. In our example, supervisor-set goals, employee-set goals, and no goal setting.
3. *Design*: Already decided — three treatment groups.
4. *Instrumentation*: In our example, Production Record Sheet, which means counting and recording number of widgets per shift per employee.
5. *Data Analysis*: This is usually a difficult part for many

dissertation writers unless well trained in design and statistics. In our example, you are comparing three groups on task performance. If assignment to groups is at random, the best bet is to use orthogonal comparisons for the two *a priori* hypotheses. If you are having difficulty with this explanation on selecting the appropriate statistics, we suggest one of the following.

1. Take a review course in statistics and/or research methodology.

2. Hire a statistician to tutor you on the statistics for your dissertation.

3. Both.

Do not rely on someone else to assume responsibility for this part of your proposal. Remember, *you* will have to defend your statistical procedures. If you don't know what the person did or why they did it, how can you possibly defend it? Some additional notes on data analysis are included in Chapter 10.

Before going on, let's summarize. The writing task cannot begin in earnest until you have roughed out the problem statement, research questions, and hypotheses. These cannot be refined until you have concurrently determined your population, defined independent/dependent variables, selected treatments and instruments, decided on assignment of subjects to groups, and planned statistical analysis procedures. *All of these key elements* can be done in a couple of pages at most, if done in rough form. From this plan of action you can then begin to write your dissertation proposal in chapter form. The following are nitty-gritty steps in a different form:

1. Identify the problem (usually from the review of literature) and make sure you have a population and reasonable control.

2. Write a draft problem statement in specific terms, including research questions. Remember that these research questions should follow logically from the problem statement you have drafted.

3. Draft testable hypotheses. Hypotheses are a *technical version* of the research questions and are stated in testable terms. Chapter 4 talks about hypotheses in more depth.

4. Develop the research design and methodology in rough form:

A. Specify selection of subjects (random or nonrandom/ from what population is this sample being drawn/by what method.)

B. Rough out treatments, including controls and form of manipulation.

C. Select instruments and data collection procedures (if subjects are to take a test, when and where will they take it and who will administer it.)

D. Define dependent/independent variables.

E. Determine the data analysis methodology.

At this point you are ready to begin writing in more detail, chapter by chapter. We strongly recommend the use of "models" for the actual writing and have included sample sections from actual dissertations.

Chapter 4

NOTES ON HYPOTHESES

Everyone seems to have trouble writing good hypotheses, so we have included some notes about the process. Well-written hypotheses are the foundation of a good study since they tell the following:

1. What groups are involved in this particular analysis. For example, goal setting vs. the no goal setting group; the combined goal setting groups vs. the no goal setting group; those scoring in the upper third on a specific measure of self concept vs. those scoring in the lower third, etc.

2. What will happen to those groups. For example, scores of goal setting group will be significantly higher than no goal setting group; there will be no significant difference between the production rates of those in the self-set goal group vs. the experimenter-set goal group.

3. How you will measure the change. For example, the average scores of the goal setting group vs. the no goal setting groups on production of widgets or on Crites Career Maturity Inventory, Attitude Scale.

Directional vs. Nondirectional vs. Null Hypotheses

An hypothesis can be stated in any one of three ways: as a directional hypothesis, as a nondirectional hypothesis, or as a null hypothesis.

When you have support from a theory and from previous research that leads you to predict a specific outcome, it makes sense to use a *directional*, or *research*, hypothesis. In this type of hypothesis, your expectations are stated as part of the hypothesis. A directional hypothesis predicts in advance what will happen to Y as a result of doing X. For example:

The mean number of errors in the production typing task performance of the moderate stress group will be significantly lower than the mean number of errors of the combined low

17

and high stress groups.

In this form, the hypothesis is a testable, clear statement of the expected relationship between two or more variables. Because it is based in both theory and previous research, it is totally defensible. The only debate here might be whether your interpretation of the theory and empirical support is reasonable and logical.

A *nondirectional* hypothesis is like the one above except that you do not specify the direction of the differences. A nondirectional hypothesis can be used when you have reason to expect differences but are not certain of the direction. In the hypothesis above, there was evidence to suggest that moderate stress usually facilitates performance while low and high stress usually inhibit performance; therefore, the writer reflected this support in the statement of the hypothesis. If, however, previous research did not support a directional statement, the hypothesis could be stated as nondirectional. For example:

> There will be a significant difference between the mean number of errors in the productional typing task performance of the moderate stress group and the mean number of errors of the combined low and high stress groups.

This hypothesis predicts a difference but does not specify which direction the difference will take.

Another type of hypothesis, found mostly in dissertations, is the *null*, or *statistical*, hypothesis. A null hypothesis allows the statisticians to compare the findings of your study against chance expectations through an appropriate statistical method. For example:

> There will be no significant differences between the mean number of errors in the production typing task performance of the moderate stress group and the mean number of errors in typing task performance of the combined low and high stress groups.

The *null* or *statistical* hypothesis is essentially the same as the directional hypotheses *except* that it states the hypothesis *exactly opposite* to what the researcher is predicting. Many traditional researchers, statisticians, and advisors insist that in dissertations the hypotheses be stated in the *null*. From a "purist" point of view this is acceptable. However, we don't recommend this approach to our students. We let the null hypothesis be understood and give preference to the research hypothesis in our text. Our point is that if the proposal writer has developed an hypothesis from an extensive review of the literature and has found both theoretical and empirical support that leads him to believe that a specific outcome will occur when X is done to Y, then it just doesn't make sense to hypothesize the opposite (except to the statistician). For the reader's sake, "say what you mean." In any event, you had better check with your advisor!

The above examples have all been concerned with differences. It should be noted that hypotheses concerned with *relationships*, that is *correlational* hypotheses, can also be stated as directional, nondirectional, or null hypotheses. For example:

DIRECTIONAL HYPOTHESIS

There will be a significant positive correlation between locus of control scores and career maturity scores.

or

There will be a significant negative correlation between locus of control scores and passivity scores.

NONDIRECTIONAL HYPOTHESIS

There will be a significant correlation between locus of control scores and career maturity scores.

NULL HYPOTHESIS

There will be no significant correlation between locus of control scores and career maturity scores.

Let's go over this procedure again. Before reading on, go back to the last chapter and reread the example on writing hypotheses from research questions.

Problem Statement Sample

Bad: This investigator will examine locus on control, goal setting, and career maturity of college women who write resumes.

Good: This study will investigate the relationship of goal setting and locus of control to career maturity in college women in a business program. Within the context of a resume writing unit of instruction, this study will be concerned with answering the following questions.

From the above problem statement, one can deduce at least four research questions and a number of hypotheses.

Research Question Sample

Bad:

1. What does resume writing do to women's career maturity?
2. What does goal setting do to women's career maturity?
3. What does goal setting do to women's performance in general?
4. What happens to locus of control and career maturity?

Good:

1. What is the effect of teaching resume writing on career maturity scores?
2. What is the effect of teaching goal-setting techniques on career maturity scores?
3. What is the effect of teaching goal-setting techniques within a specific setting upon the level of performance on a professionally related motor task outside the setting?
4. What is the relationship between locus of control scores (self-reported and teacher rated) and career maturity scores?

Note: The use of the word *scores* is important. We can't see what happens to "career maturity" since it is only an abstraction. We can see what happens to test scores.

From the good research questions you can write testable hypotheses. The following are examples of good and bad testable hypotheses for research question number 2:

Bad: The women getting training in goal setting will be more mature than those who just write resumes by the end of the course.

Good: Within the context of resume writing, the mean scores of the goal setting group will be significantly higher than the mean scores of the no goal setting group on the following measures of the Crites Career Maturity Inventory (1973): 1) Competence Test, Part 3 — Choosing a Job and 2) Competence

Test, Part 4 — Looking Ahead.

This hypothesis is a testable one. You can compare the mean (average) scores of the groups on a test. The independent variable is obviously something to do with goal setting and the dependent variables are subtests of a standardized test.

Hypotheses Should Be Supported

Hypotheses should be supported from theory and/or research. You should be able to say "Based on this theory and supported by these studies" this hypothesis makes sense. Many advisors want both theoretical and empirical support for hypotheses and most of the examples given in the later sections of the guidebook are written with such support. This doesn't mean that "clinical hunches" should be ignored. However, it is our opinion that hypotheses that are written in testable form and are supported by previous empirical studies and deduced from theory are easier to defend and are more likely to lead to significant outcomes. Save your "fishing expeditions" for post-doctoral work.

For a further discussion of hypotheses, see Chapter 8.

SUMMARY CHECK SHEET

DIRECTIONS: Our suggestion is that you briefly rough out the following steps (if you have not already done so).

1. Draft a brief description of your treatment(s) if you are doing an experimental or quasi-experimental design.

2. Define your independent variable(s) briefly.

3. Describe your instruments and data collection procedures.

4. Define your dependent variable(s).

5. Write a draft of your problem statement.

6. List your research questions.

7. Draft testable hypotheses.

8. Make a sketch of your design and data analysis procedures (see Chapters 9, 10, and 11).

9. Describe the population and assignment to conditions or treatments.

List as many details of your methodology and procedures that need to be refined as you can. Use short phrases and key words to outline the proposal. Once this is complete, begin writing section by section using the models of actual dissertations and dissertation proposals provided on the following pages. Good luck!

HELPFUL REFERENCES

Research and Theory

Ary, D., Jacobs, L. and Razavieh, A. *Introduction to research in education.* New York, HR&W, 1972.

Best, J. *Research in education.* Englewood Cliffs, NJ, P-H, 1970.

Campbell, D. and Stanley, J. *Experimental and quasi-experimental designs for research.* Chicago, Rand, 1963.

Cook, T. D. and Campbell, D. T. *Quasi-experimentation: design & analysis for field settings.* Chicago, Rand, 1979.

Isaac, S. *Handbook in research and evaluation.* San Diego, CA, EDITS, 1977.

Keppel. G. *Design and analysis: A researcher's handbook.* Englewood Cliffs, NJ, P-H, 1973.

Kerlinger, F. *Foundations of behavioral research.* New York, HR&W, 1964.

Nunnally, J. *Psychometric theory.* New York, McGraw, 1978.

Webb, E., Campbell, D., Schwartz, R., and Sechrest, L. *Unobtrusive measures: Nonreactive research in the social sciences.* Chicago, Rand, 1966.

Weiss, C. *Evaluation research.* Englewood Cliffs, NJ, P-H, 1972.

Statistics

Guilford, J. and Fruchter, B. *Fundamental statistics in psychology and education.* New York, McGraw, 1978.

Kerlinger, F. and Pedhazur, E. *Multiple regression in behavioral research.* New York, HR&W, 1973.

Kleinbaum, D. and Kupper, L. *Applied regression analysis and other multivariable methods.* North Scituate, MA: Duxbury Pr, 1978.

Siegel, S. *Nonparametric statistics for the behavioral sciences.* New York, McGraw, 1956.

Roscoe, J. *Fundamental research statistics.* New York, HR&W, 1969.

Dissertation Models

Cowan, G. J. *The Effects of Teaching Goal Setting Procedures on the Career Maturity and Classroom Performance of Business College Women Differing in Locus of Control.* Doctoral dissertation, Boston University, 1979.

Curry, J. *The Effects of Life Planning Instruction and Career Counseling on Locus of Control Orientation and Career Maturity Scores of University Compensatory Education Students.* Doctoral dissertation, Boston University, 1980.

Dewey, B. *Factors Affecting Initial Employment in Special Education.* Doctoral dissertation, Boston University, 1979.

Gardner, D. C. *Goal Setting, Locus of Control and Work Performance of Mentally Retarded Adults.* Doctoral dissertation, Boston University, 1974.

Grossman, B. J. *The Effects of Decision-making Skill Instruction on Locus of Control, Career Choice Competency, and Occupational Information Seeking Behavior.* Doctoral dissertation, Boston University, 1979.

Kurtz, M. *The Effects of Goal Setting and Anxiety on Accuracy of Production Typing Task Performance.* Doctoral dissertation, Boston University, 1978.

Section II

Models

In this writing business, a man necessarily becomes his own master, sets his own pace, becomes his own taskmaster. To a large extent he accomplishes what he thinks he can accomplish, and invariably fails to accomplish what he feels he cannot accomplish.

Erle Stanley Gardner

This section offers "models" for you to use in writing your proposal. Many universities, colleges, and departments have specific guidelines about how the proposal or dissertation should be organized. Although there is nothing sacrosanct about any of the traditionally accepted formats, it is your responsibility to determine which one is preferred by your advisor and to follow it.

We prefer that the Review of the Literature appear as an appendix and to state the hypotheses and their theoretical and empirical support in Chapter 2. It should be noted that there is a difference between a statement of theoretical and empirical support and a review of the literature. In the former, you cite those studies which support your hypotheses, treatment, etc. In the latter, you may choose to discuss additional studies which relate to your topic. You should also critique the studies in the review of literature, something you don't do in the theoretical and empirical support section.

In any case, all quality dissertations contain the same elements. In our opinion the order of the headings and chapters is relatively unimportant as long as the text is emminently readable and in logical order.

Chapter 5

SAMPLE INTRODUCTION, BACKGROUND OF THE PROBLEM, STATEMENT OF THE PROBLEM, AND RESEARCH QUESTIONS

SAMPLE 1

A N "Introduction" section from an alumni follow-up study.*

Changing economic conditions and birth patterns have altered drastically the career opportunities of many professionals in recent years. This is particularly evident in the teaching profession. The National Education Association (1977) forecasts a significant decrease in the school age population for the next two decades.

> The age 5-13 group dropped or will drop between 2.0 and 2.6 percent in 1973, 1974, and in 1977 through 1979. . . . The years in which the percentage drop in the age 14-17 population will exceed 2.0 percent are from 1979 through 1983, and from 1987 through 1989. . . .
> The age 18-21 population will decline by 2.0 percent or more each year between 1983 and 1987, and between 1991 and 1993. . . . The drop of 4 million persons in this age group between its peak of 17,137,000 in 1979 to the 1994 low is about one-fourth (23.3 percent) of the total number of this age group in 1979 (p. 36).

In spite of declining school enrollments, there is a need for

---

*The "Introduction/Background of the Problem" section does not need to be more than 3 to 5 pages in length, as in Samples 1 and 3. Get your thoughts well organized before writing this section. Think of it as a "lead-in" to your problem statement, a short overview which places your readers squarely in the middle and context of the current research/theory/needs in the field from which you have deduced your problem. *Don't* review all the literature here: that is a common mistake. Get to the point. This section should lead logically, simply, and directly to the formal Statement of the Problem section.

"new" teachers each year (N.E.A., 1977). New teachers are defined by the National Education Association as "a person entering or reentering active status who was not employed as a full-time teacher during the preceding school year" (p. 5). However: "The number of prospective teachers from the 1976 graduating class seeking teaching positions (185,850) exceeds by 91,700 the number of teaching positions actually open to them" (p. 5).

Under these conditions, teacher training institutions may need to place more emphasis on the career development education of their clientele. For instance, in what way should preservice teachers be counseled to ensure that they have greater opportunity (because of skills provided by the college) to enter a career in teaching after graduation?

The alumni of any teacher training program can be divided into two groups: (a) employed as trained and (b) not employed as trained. This study focused on a sample of graduates to determine if total grade point average, grade point average in professional courses, use of a placement file, total Scholastic Achievement Test scores, Scholastic Achievement Verbal Test scores, and Scholastic Achievement Mathematics Test scores were related to obtainment of employment in the field for which trained. The area of Special Education was chosen because that area is still one in which demand is relatively high, because the options for moving into other related areas is relatively high, and because a sample of sufficient size was available from a single program with a Bachelor of Science degree.

SAMPLE 2

A "Statement of the Problem/Research Questions" section from an alumni follow-up study.*

---

*A "Statement of the Problem" section should be crystal clear to the reader. The reader should have absolutely no difficulty in understanding *exactly* what you plan to study. Most graduate students make the mistake of writing a problem statement which is much too broad in scope. Remember, your approach is to employ a rifle, not a shotgun, to get at the larger problem. Don't fall into the trap of thinking that your study must be THE definitive work on the topic! A good study, based on a rifle-shot approach to the Statement of the Problem, adds one small piece to a complex puzzle

→

The major focus of this study was to examine grade point average, Scholastic Achievement Test scores, and establishment of a placement file in an attempt to determine if these variables were related to employment in the field for which a student is trained.

Within the context of success or failure in obtained employment as a special education teacher, this study was concerned with the following major question and related corollary questions:

Major Question:

Which, if any, of the six variables examined will be related to employment in the field of special education?

Corollary Questions:

1. Is there a relationship between total grade point average obtained in college and employment status?
2. Is there a relationship between grade point average in professional courses completed in college and employment status?
3. Is there a relationship between the total of the Verbal and Mathematics scores of the Scholastic Achievement Test and employment status?
4. Is there a relationship between the Verbal score of the Scholastic Achievement Test and employment status?
5. Is there a relationship between the Mathematics score of the Scholastic Achievement Test and employment status?
6. Is there a relationship between the establishment of a placement file and employment status?

---

about some aspect of human behavior.

"Research Questions" are naturally and logically deduced from the problem statement. Note in Samples 2 and 4 how the research questions just seem to make sense and how they naturally "flow" from the problem statement. The combination of the declarative Problem Statement and the Research Questions serve to focus the study on specific goals. Research Questions deduced from the Problem Statement serve to further define and limit the scope of the problem. Research Questions normally suggest "cause and effect" or significant relationships. They may suggest anwers to questions and should lead to the formulation of hypotheses.

SAMPLE 3

An "Introduction/Background of the Problem" section from a quasi-experimental design study.

In his own summary of the work of the O'Toole Task Force (*Work In America*, 1973), Super (1976) underscores the importance of work in our modern society: "Work is central in the lives of most adults, it contributes to identity and self-esteem, and it is useful in bringing order and meaning into life. Work offers economic self-sufficiency, status, family stability, and an opportunity to interact with others in one of the most basic activities of society."

Thus, work is more than just a means to obtain a livelihood in our culture; it influences every aspect of our lives including personality development. "Our society needs to accept the importance of work as it relates to both the economic and psychological well-being of each citizen. . . . The rationale . . . is rooted in the simple fact that each individual's own self concept is intimately related to what that individual does for a living" (Gardner & Warren, 1978, p. 27).

The transition from school to work represents a milestone in the lives of most youth. To the extent that the educational process can facilitate this transition, the schools will have made a major contribution to the well-being of the individual and to society as a whole. For most workers, the transitional period for moving from school to work is between ages 16 and 25. This marks the beginning of the Establishment stage (Super, 1953), the most critical stage of career development, during which the die is often cast for a career of success or failure (Crites, 1976).

Fortunately, career development can be guided (Crites, 1973b, 1976; Super, 1953; Tiedeman, 1961). To the extent that "thwarting conditions" are effectively handled, the career development of the young adult, for both the present *and* the future, may be more or less facilitated (Crites, 1976). Due to the developmental nature of the process, success at a prior stage is a powerful predictor of future adaptation.

. . . As Havighurst (1953) has observed, success with earlier developmental tasks is related to success with later ones. It would be expected, therefore that . . . students in the Exploratory stage who were most career mature in their choice attitudes and competencies would be better career adjusted during the transition from school to work. Similarly, the neophyte workers who coped relatively effectively with the problems of job entry should become established more firmly during the induction process (Crites, 1976, p. 108).

Since career maturity seems to be a major determinant for future occupational success, it appears to be a logical point for instructional interventions. Since career maturity is a multidimensional personality construct, it lends itself to didactic intervention at those points where it overlaps Social Learning Theory (Rotter, 1975).

SAMPLE 4

A "Statement of the Problem/Research Questions" section from a quasi-experimental design study.

A key component of definitions of career maturity is an emphasis on goal-directed behavior. A career mature person is seen as one who can select *goals* for himself which are consistent with his or her own capabilities (Crites, 1973) and who is *goal-directed* (Bohn, 1966). Consequently,

If one begins to read the literature concerned with how people set goals and goal-directed behavior, one is initially overwhelmed by the sheer volume of reports which have been published on the topic since the early 1930s. On the basis of the volume of attention given the subject, one can conclude that the study of goals, goal-setting and goal-directed behavior is an important one to psychologists and educators (Gardner & Warren, 1978, p. 104).

It is at this juncture, the emphasis on the study of goal-directed behaviors, that career development theory logically comes into juxtaposition with that portion of social learning theory that is concerned with level of aspiration or goal setting.

The study of goal setting lends itself to exploration through the application of Rotter's theory: "The occurrence of a behavior of a person is determined not only by the nature or importance of the goals or reinforcements but also by the person's anticipation or expectancy that these goals will occur" (Rotter, 1954, p. 102).

Moreover, this behavior ". . . depends upon whether or not the person perceives a causal relationship between his own behavior and the reward" (Rotter, 1966, p. 1).

As a result, one's behavior is seen as affected not only by the nature or importance of the goals or reinforcements involved (Gardner, 1974b) but by the

> . . . degree to which an individual . . . accepts responsibility for the outcomes of his or her own behavior. A person who believes that what happens to him is a result of his own behavior is said to have an "internal locus of control." Conversely, a person who believes that what happens to him is a matter of "luck," "chance," or the whims of "powerful others" is said to have an external locus of control (Gardner & Warren, 1978, p. 89).

What this means is that persons who have a heightened expectancy for reinforcement because of goal setting will be more likely to perform better than persons not setting goals. Furthermore, persons who *believe* that what happens to them is of their own doing (internals) will be more likely to perform better than peers who do not see the connection between the rewards they receive and their own behavior (externals). Thus, one can deduce from career development theory and social learning theory that there should be a logical relationship between the effects of, goal setting and career maturity and between a person's locus of control and career maturity.

The literature on locus of control and goal setting is extensive (Gardner, 1974b; Kurtz, 1978; Gardner & Warren, 1978). There are a number of recent studies concerned with locus of control and career maturity (Gable, 1973; Ifenwanta, 1978; Thomas, 1974; Wilson, 1975; and Wilton, 1978). However, a review of the literature revealed a dearth of studies on goal setting as an independent variable and its effects on career maturity. While many studies have been concerned with the topics of level of aspiration and/or locus of control, none have focused on studying the effects of goal setting and locus of control on career maturity.

This study will investigate the relationship of goal setting and locus of control to career maturity in college women in a business program. Within the context of a resume writing unit of instruction, this study will be concerned with the following questions:

1. What is the effect of teaching resume writing on career maturity scores?
2. What is the effect of teaching goal-setting techniques on career maturity scores?
3. What is the effect of teaching goal-setting techniques within a specific setting upon level of performance on a professionally-related motor task outside of the setting?
4. What is the relationship between locus of control scores (self-reported and teacher-rated) and career maturity scores?

Chapter 6

SAMPLE JUSTIFICATION OR SIGNIFICANCE OF THE PROBLEM, LIMITATIONS, AND ASSUMPTIONS

SAMPLE 5

"JUSTIFICATION/Assumptions/Limitations" sections from a quasi-experimental design study.*

This study drew on two theoretical fields, social learning theory and career development theory, in an effort to test a didactic intervention to "increase (career) maturity . . . and presumably, therefore, enhanc(e) the success with which training and work tasks can be accomplished" (Crites, 1976, p. 109). To that end, this study focused on three areas of importance: goal setting, locus of control, and career maturity.

---

*While each "Justification, or Significance, of the Problem" section is an individually thought out statement explaining how the proposed study will increase knowledge, most have common elements:

1. An explanation of how the findings will contribute to on-going research in the topic area.
2. An explanation of how the findings will contribute to theory (where appropriate).
3. A statement of how the new or increased knowledge may help to improve practice in the field.
4. If required by your department, a statement about how your experience and training qualify you to do the study.

Assumptions and Limitations describe factors that may affect the outcomes of the study or are important to interpretation of the findings. In both cases, these are factors over which you have no *absolute* control. For instance, your study's findings are limited in their generalizability to the "type of population" you choose to study. You cannot generalize to a population of cats if you study mice. Moreover, in interpreting your findings, you always start with your assumptions. You assume "no extreme personality differences" and therefore attribute changes to the "treatment." In fact, extreme personality differences may offer an alternative explanation for the findings and you may want to check it out.

34

The literature on goal setting, locus of control, and career maturity as individual constructs is extensive. A review of literature by von Esch found over a thousand studies and articles on locus of control, "the vast majority of which had been completed subsequent to Rotter's 1966 monograph" (1978, p. 105). This investigation studied goal setting as an independent variable and its effects on career maturity scores. It also investigated the relationship of locus of control, goal setting, and career maturity.

A review of the literature has also revealed a dearth of studies on the transference of goal-setting behavior to tasks outside of the study. One might hypothesize that this would occur based on studies by James (1957), but there have been no investigations that have studied it directly. This study investigated the transference of goal-setting behavior as it relates to locus of control.

The findings of this study should contribute to a better understanding of the relationship of locus of control, goal setting, and career maturity as they relate to young women preparing to enter the world of work. They also add to the growing body of knowledge in two important fields, career development and social learning, as well as the body of knowledge concerned with the degree of congruence of both fields.

Additionally, if it is true, as career development theory postulates, that "those individuals who were more career-mature in their decision making during the Exploratory stage would be better adjusted (more satisfied and successful) in the initial years of the Establishment stage than those who were less career-mature in their choices before occupational entry" (Crites, 1976, p. 112), then the findings of this study may have immediate practical application as an educational intervention technique for affecting career maturity and consequently successful adjustment to the world of work.

Limitations of the Study

1. All of the persons in this study were students in a single two-year college. Thus, generalizations of the findings to other populations or settings may not be appropriate.

2. Only two tasks, resume writing and typing, were used in this study. Generalizations from performance on these tasks to other tasks may be limited, even under similar conditions.

3. It is possible that "experimenter" effects may account for any differences that may be found.

Assumptions

1. It was assumed that there were no extreme differences in ability or personality in the groups being tested.

2. It was assumed that the experimenter's behavior in each of the treatment groups did not differ except in those areas that distinguished between treatments.

SAMPLE 6

"Justification/Assumptions/Limitation" sections from a *true experimental design study.*

Northeastern University expended $250,000 during the 1978-1979 budget year on compensatory education programs. It is anticipated that $450,000 will be spent in 1979-1980 with 20 percent of entering freshmen (800 students) involved in some aspect of the total compensatory offerings — Writing, Reading, Study Skills, or Mathematics.

The largest private university and the largest cooperative education institution in the country, Northeastern will be particularly impacted by the success or lack of same achieved by these marginal students. Commencing with the sophomore year, Northeastern students become involved in the Co-operative Plan of Education, whereby they alternate periods of paid employment directly related to careers with their academic programs.

Implications of this study go far beyond Northeastern University. As mentioned earlier, many colleges and universities are expending resources on underprepared students. The findings of this study will have implications for other universities and may lead them to alter their programs to include more than academic offerings should the treatments prove to be effective.

Thirdly, this study will make a contribution to Social Learning Theory. A review of the literature indicates that, to this date, no one has attempted to modify the locus of control of this particular population, the newly arrived compensatory student in higher education. In addition, this study will contribute to the growing body of literature on Career Development Theory.

Finally, the findings of this study may provide a better understanding of the relationship of life planning instruction to both locus of control and career maturity as they affect a population of paramount importance to higher education — a population with which they have not dealt in such large numbers in the past, a population critical to the schools as we enter the 1980s.

Limitations

1. Subjects will be freshmen compensatory education students at one urban university. Generalizations of the findings are limited to those institutions who enroll students with similar backgrounds.

2. It is possible that experimenter effects may account for any differences that may be found.

3. The fact that treatments will be offered at different times during the day may affect the findings.

Assumptions

1. It is assumed that there will be no extreme differences in personality in the groups being tested.

2. It is assumed that the behavior of the professionals in each of the treatment groups will not differ except in those areas that distinguish between treatments.

SAMPLE 7

"Justification" section from an alumni follow-up study.

A review of the literature revealed several studies (e.g. Dipboye, Fromkin, & Wiback, 1975) that have investigated the relationship of grade point average, placement files, and Scholastic Achievement Test scores to employment. However, no major studies were found that have attempted to determine if there was a significant relationship between the variables in this study and the obtainment of a position in special education. This study was conducted to determine if there was a relationship between the variables listed and employment in special education in today's job market.

The results of this study have implications for career training in a broad perspective. The results also have implications for persons concerned with the planning of career development activities that should be integrated into the ongoing teacher training program of universities and colleges (Hoyt, 1975).

This study can be used by advisors, counseling and placement personnel, students, and others interested in career development. The findings of this study can be useful in career planning, academic advising, preparation of placement files, and planning for effective and meaningful academic programs.

Chapter 7

SAMPLE DEFINITIONS OF OPERATIONAL TERMS

SAMPLE 8

"DEFINITIONS of Operational Terms"
*from a quasi-experimental design study.**

Career Maturity Inventory (CMI) refers to the instrument developed by Crites (1973) to evaluate the level of maturity of attitudes and competencies required for career decision-making. The Inventory has two parts: an Attitude Scale and a Competence Test.

Competence Test, Part 5 — What Should They Do refers to the fifth subtest of the Competence Test of the Career Maturity Inventory.

Decision-Making Skill for the purposes of this dissertation is defined as (1) career choice competency as measured by Crites Career Maturity Inventory, Competence Test, Part 5 — What Should They Do (Crites, 1973), and (2) level of occupational information-seeking behavior as measured by the Vocational Checklist (Aiken & Cox, 1970a).

Different Situations Inventory (DSI) refers to an instrument designed to measure locus of control developed by

---

*The purpose of the "Definitions of Operational Terms" section is to get everybody talking the same language. If "my old man/lady" means father/mother to you and something quite different to me, you and I may draw inferences about each other's behavior which may be erroneous. In understanding, interpreting, and communicating research information on human beings, it is imperative that we all operate on the same "wave length."

All variables in your study should be clearly, concisely, and unambiguously defined in operational terms. If one of your variables is "career maturity," then it should be defined in the terms in which you plan to measure it. See Samples 8 and 10 for approaches. If one of your variables is "achievement," explain what you mean by achievement in measurable terms. You may define achievement in any number of ways, for instance, a score on a standardized academic achievement test, a grade in a course, the number of dollar sales, etc.

Gardner and Warren (1978). The Self-Report Form is a version of the Different Situations Inventory in which the subject is asked to answer questions about himself.

Locus of Control (LC) refers " . . . to a person's belief about the degree to which reinforcements are contingent upon his own behavior. Persons who believe that reinforcements are contingent upon their own behavior, capacities, or attributes are said to have an *internal locus of control (ILC)*. Persons who believe that reinforcements are not under their personal control but rather are under the control of powerful others or may be attributed to 'luck,' 'chance' or 'fate' are said to have an *external locus of control (ELC)*" (Gardner, 1974, p. 8).

Student, subject refers to the persons taking part in this study.

Vocational Checklist refers to an instrument developed by Aiken and Cox (1970a) to measure specific occupational information-seeking behaviors. This instrument is comprised of two scales: the *Cognitive Scale*, which measures instances that the student thought about, or internally evaluated information, and the *Behavioral Scale*, which measures instances that the student actively, physically sought out information. In this dissertation, the term *Vocational Checklist* refers only to the *Behavioral Scale*.

SAMPLE 9

"Definition of Operational Terms" from an alumni follow-up study.

Employment refers to services exchanged for monetary reward. In this study employment specifically refers to the full-time employment, after graduating with a Bachelor of Science degree in Special Education, in the field of special education.

Special Education refers to a specialized form of education that focuses on handicapped children, those children evaluated as being mentally retarded, hard of hearing, deaf, speech impaired, visually handicapped, seriously emotionally disturbed, orthopedically impaired, other health impaired, deaf-blind, multi-handicapped or as having specific learning disabilities, who because of those impairments need special education and related services.

Special Education teacher refers to individuals who are formally trained in a college or university to teach and who are eligible for certification by the Massachusetts Department of Education as being qualified to teach a particular grade level or subject.

Related Special Education Services refers to transportation and such developmental, corrective, and other supportive services as are required to assist a handicapped child to benefit from special education, and includes speech pathology, audiology, psychological services, physical and occupational therapy, recreation, early identification and assessment of disabilities in children, counseling services, medical services for diagnostic and evaluation purposes, school health services, social work services in schools and parent counseling and training (U.S. Public Law 94-142).

SAT Scores refers to scores obtained on the Scholastic Achievement Test when the student was a senior in high school. In this study it refers to the combined and separate mathematics and verbal components of the test.

SAMPLE 10

"Definitions of Operational Terms" from quasi-experimental design study.

Business Communications refers to a college course which deals with oral and written communications as they relate to the business world.

Career Maturity refers to the level of an individual's career development in relation to his age (Crites, 1973b, p. 7). In this study, career maturity refers to the measurable outcomes of the career development process as defined by Crites' Career Maturity Inventory, Parts 3 and 4 of the Competence Test.

Career Maturity Inventory (CMI) refers to the instrument developed by Crites (1973a) to evaluate the level of career maturity.

Different Situations Inventory (DSI) refers to a locus of control instrument developed by Gardner & Warren (1978). The *Self-*

Report Form is a version of the Different Situations Inventory in which the subject answers questions about himself. The *Teacher-Report Form* (Rating Form) is a version of the Different Situations Inventory in which a rater answers questions about another person.

Goal Setting refers to the act of expressing, either verbally or in writing, an expected performance level. *Long-term goal setting* refers to the act of expressing, either verbally or in writing, an expected level of performance for one year and for five years from the present. *Short-term goal setting* refers to the act of expressing, either verbally or in writing, an expected level of performance for an immediate task.

Chapter 8

SAMPLE CORRELATIONAL HYPOTHESES, HYPOTHESES FROM TRUE EXPERIMENTAL AND QUASI-EXPERIMENTAL DESIGNS, AND THEORETICAL AND EMPIRICAL FRAMEWORK

SAMPLE 11

"CORRELATIONAL Hypotheses" from an alumni follow-up study.

Hypothesis Number 1. There will be a significant positive correlation between total grade point average and employment in the field of special education.

Hypothesis Number 2. There will be a significant positive correlation between grade point average in professional courses and employment in the field of special education.

Hypothesis Number 3. There will be a significant positive correlation between Scholastic Achievement Verbal Test scores and employment in the field of special education.

Hypothesis Number 4. There will be a significant positive correlation between Scholastic Achievement Mathematics Test scores and employment in the field of special education.

Hypothesis Number 5. There will be a significant positive

You may want to review Chapter 4 before reading these three examples. Remember that hypotheses may be stated in a number of ways. No matter your preference or your advisor's preference for format, a good hypothesis must (1) be stated in the simplest, clearest form possible; (2) be *testable* as stated; (3) be reasonable and rational; (4) be consistent with the research in the field; and (5) be consistent with current theory.

An hypothesis is your educated guess or hunch in answer to a question. Your study's objective is to collect data in such a fashion that you will be able to confirm or disconfirm your hypothesis.

correlation between total Scholastic Achievement Test scores (verbal plus mathematics) and employment in the field of special education.

Hypothesis Number 6. There will be a significant positive correlation between establishment of a Boston University placement file and employment in the field of special education.

SAMPLE 12

"Hypotheses and Theoretical Support" sections from a true experimental design.

The hypotheses which follow are presented with theoretical support derived from Rotter's Social Learning Theory (1954, 1966, 1972, 1975) and Career Development Theory (Super, 1953, 1957; Crites, 1969, 1976; Tiedeman, 1961). Empirical support for the hypotheses was drawn from relevant research reports.

Hypotheses Related to Locus of Control Orientation

Hypothesis 1 — The mean locus of control scores, as measured by the Different Situations Inventory Self-Report Form (Gardner and Warren, 1978) of the groups receiving instruction in *life planning* will be significantly higher (thus more internal) than the mean of the no treatment group.

Hypothesis 2 — The mean locus of control scores as measured by the Different Situations Inventory, Self-Report Form (Gardner and Warren, 1978) of the group receiving *life planning instruction and the career counseling component* will be significantly higher (thus more internal) than the mean of the *life planning group.*

Hypothesis 3 — There will be a significant positive correlation between locus of control scores, as measured by the Self-Report Form of the Different Situations Inventory (Gardner and Warren, 1978) and Parts 3, 4, 5 of the Career Maturity Inventory (Crites, 1973).

1. Competence Test, Part 3 — Choosing A Job
2. Competence Test, Part 4 — Looking Ahead
3. Competence Test, Part 5 — What Should I Do?

Theoretical Support for Hypotheses 1, 2, 3

One of the major postulates of Rotter's Social Learning Theory (1954, 1966, 1972, 1975) is the personality construct of *locus of control*. Locus of control

> . . . refers to the degree to which an individual person (e.g., a student, a worker) accepts responsibility for the outcomes of his or her own behavior. A person who believes that what happens to him is a result of his own behavior is said to have an "internal locus of control." Conversely, a person who believes that what happens to him is a matter of "luck," "chance," or the whims of "powerful others," is said to have an "external locus of control." (Gardner and Warren, 1978, p. 89).

A. P. MacDonald, Jr. (1972) states that those individuals with an internal locus of control really believe that they can effect change in their lives; therefore, they work toward desired objectives. In contrast, those individuals with an external locus of control do not perceive a relationship between their behavior and outcomes; therefore, they are less likely to extend effort to bring about desired objectives or goals or accomplishments and are less likely to try to solve problems.

Other Social Learning theorists (Phares, 1976; Lefcourt and Ludwig, 1965) have postulated that locus of control can be modified through a number of procedures. Gardner and Warren (1978) have developed an instructional design model for modifying locus of control (see Figure 1).

Gardner and Warren (1978) propose that: ". . . An individual's locus of control can be changed from external to internal through involvement in an educational program which is designed to teach a person to see the relationship between his or her own behavior and the reinforcements he or she receives" (p. 19).

Thus, it is predicted that students in this study who undertake the life planning course with units concerned with Cooperative Education, Career Information, Self-Assessment, Resume Writing, Decision Making, Goal Setting, Problem Solving, and the Interview and those students who receive this treatment as well as the career counseling component designed

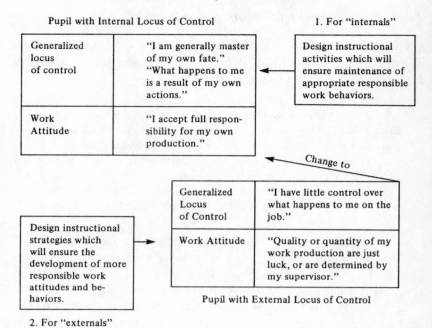

Figure 1. Instructional Design Model. Reprinted from D. C. Gardner and S. A. Warren, *Careers and Disabilities: A Career Education Approach* (Stanford, Conn.: Greylock Publishers, Inc., 1978), with permission of authors and publisher.

to change locus of control towards a more internal orientation will experience changes in locus of control scores. That instruction in life planning skills and a life planning/career counseling component will affect locus of control is logical. Learning life planning skills by definition involves the following process: clarifying values, setting objectives based on values, and planning future actions necessary to achieve desired goals. One can hypothesize that the strategies postulated by MacDonald (1972) and Dua (1970) to be effective techniques in helping individuals to recognize the contingency relationship between behavior and reinforcement will help modify locus of control orientation.

The intersection of locus of control and career maturity occurs in goal directedness and reality orientation. Cowan (1979) theorized that at that point in Career Development Theory where the study of goal-directed behaviors is tantamount, Social Learning Theory logically comes into juxtaposition. Thus, the proposed activities of this study have a double-edged theoretical base.

An important aspect of life planning instruction is learning through case studies. Gardner and Gardner (1974) stress that the use of case studies which emphasize the contingency relationship between behavior and outcome should affect locus of control.

In addition, it is hypothesized from Social Learning Theory that students presented with the opportunity to plan for the future in order to attain their objectives should logically raise their expectations of effecting the desired outcomes. Such expectations for effecting desired outcomes are theoretically associated with Rotter's internal locus of control orientation (Rotter, 1975).

SAMPLE 13

"Hypotheses, Theoretical and Empirical Support" sections from a study consisting of two quasi-experimental designs run simultaneously.*

The following hypotheses are presented with theoretical and empirical support. Theoretical support was deduced from Rotter's Social Learning Theory (1954, 1972, 1975) or Spielberger's (1966, 1970) state-trait conception of anxiety. Empirical support was drawn from relevant research reports.

Students sometimes get confused between "Theoretical Support" and "Empirical Support" for an hypothesis. While theories of human behavior are built on empirical data, there is a difference between the two ways of thinking. A theory is a *comprehensive explanation* of a phenomenon. In learning theory, for instance, Rotter's Social Learning Theory is a comprehensive explanation of how people learn from other people and why they behave as they do as a result of this learning. From such a comprehensive explanation of learning and behavior one can deduce or predict how people will behave or learn under certain conditions.

In contrast, empirical support consists of studies which test the theory with different populations under different conditions. You should use empirical support to justify the different elements of your study, for instance, the type of treatment, the length of the treatment, the population, etc.

Hypotheses for Experiment I (Goal Setting)

Hypothesis 1a. The mean number of errors of the three treatment groups (self set, experimenter set, no goal set) will differ significantly.

Hypothesis 1b. There will be no significant differences in mean number of errors between the two goal setting groups (self set vs. experimenter set).

Hypothesis 1c. The mean number of errors in the combined goal setting groups will be significantly lower than the mean number of errors of the no goal setting group.

Theoretical Support for Hypothesis on Goal Setting

Rotter's Social Learning Theory (1954) states: "The occurrence of a behavior of a person is determined not only by the nature or importance of the goals or reinforcement but also by the person's anticipation or expectancy that these goals will occur" (p. 102).

According to this theory, the act of "goal setting," whether set by the student or by the experimenter, will increase the student's expectancy or anticipation that such behavior will occur. Thus it was predicted that the procedure of setting a goal would increase a student's expectancy that the behavior (e.g., "accuracy") will occur and will motivate the student to direct greater effort toward obtaining the predicted goal (accuracy).

Empirical Support for Hypothesis 1a, 1b, and 1c

Four studies on goal setting as an independent variable found that goal setting subjects significantly performed better than no goal setting peers on both motor tasks and cognitive tasks. (See Gardner, 1974; Moreland, 1977).

Hypotheses for Experiment II (Anxiety)

Hypothesis 2a. The mean number of errors in the production typing task performance of three treatment groups (low, moderate, and high stress) will differ significantly.

Hypothesis 2b. The mean number of errors in the production typing task performance of the moderate stress group will be significantly lower than the mean number of errors of the low and high stress groups combined.

Hypothesis 2c. The mean A-State scores of those scoring high on the A-Trait scale will differ significantly from the mean A-State scale scores of those scoring low or moderate on the A-Trait scale.

Theoretical Support for Hypotheses on Anxiety

Since Spielberger (1966) theorizes that varying degrees of anxiety will affect task performance, it was hypothesized that the three groups in the three levels of stress (low, moderate, and high) would differ significantly in the number of errors made on the production typing task performance test. Moreover, since Spielberger postulates that the moderate anxiety facilitates task performance, it was predicted that a moderate amount of (stress) anxiety would increase the accuracy of students on the production typing task performance.

Empirical Support for Hypotheses on Anxiety

Three studies of college age students on task performance (O'Niel, Spielberger, and Hansen, 1969; O'Neil, Hansen, and Spielberger, 1969; and O'Neil, 1969) found that error rate differed under varying degrees of stress. Grinker and Spiegel (1945) observed that moderate anxiety caused increased and more efficient activity to those experiencing the holocaust of war. Spielberger (1962) found the high anxious students were academic failures at all levels of ability except the highest. Spielberger (1966) also reported on a study undertaken in 1955 in which high anxious students reported "choking" or "blocking" in test situations. Nixon (1969) found that students who scored high on the A-Trait scale also scored high on the A-State scale.

Chapter 9

SAMPLE METHODOLOGY FOR EXPERIMENTAL DESIGNS AND METHODOLOGY FOR A FOLLOW-UP SURVEY

SAMPLE 14

"METHODOLOGY" section from a true experimental design study.*

---

*Each study is unique and therefore your methodology chapter will be different from all others. However, all methodology chapters have common elements. The approach is always the same: TO DESCRIBE IN DETAIL exactly what you plan to do, with whom you plan to do it, and how you plan to do it. The methodology chapter is best viewed as a RECIPE that anyone should be able to duplicate. If you leave out the smallest detail, your study is not replicable.

As we said in the beginning, the *Guidebook* is not a complete work on dissertation writing since the scope of such a work would indeed be formidable. However, in this Chapter we have presented two "Methodology" examples. We chose first a "true experimental design" in which the author had control of almost every conceivable variable. The hypotheses were based in theory and previous research, and the major hypotheses were supported by the results of the study.

We make this point here to show our bias. We think the best dissertation is an experimental one that contributes to theory and adds to previous work in the same area. We agree with Ary, Jacobs and Razavieh (1972): "Experimentation is the most rigorous and the most desirable form of scientific inquiry. The controlled conditions that characterize the experiment make it possible to identify verified functional relationships among the phenomena of interest . . ." (p. 261).

Unfortunately, all problems in education, psychology, and other social sciences do not lend themselves to experimental work. We have therefore included the methodology section from a follow-up survey study because the use of questionnaires or surveys is one of the most widely used techniques in educational research (Isaac, 1971). The questionnaire technique is also one of the most abused techniques in human research. Too many of the people flooding the mails with questionnaires don't bother to find out how to design a good survey or questionnaire. The sample in this section is an excellent example of how to design a questionnaire that gives reliable and valid answers to the specific research hypotheses of the study.

50

1. Institutional Setting

Located in Boston, Northeastern University is the largest private university in the country with 34,910 students studying full-time or part-time for degrees and another 16,120 enrolled in certificate programs.

Northeastern University was founded in 1898 as an extension of the Boston YMCA. It is incorporated as a privately endowed nonsectarian institution of higher learning under the General Laws of Massachusetts.

A distinctive feature of Northeastern University is its Cooperative Plan. This educational method enables students to gain valuable practical experience as an integral part of their college programs and also provides the means by which they may contribute substantially to the financing of their education.

The college site of this investigation is University College, the unit to which compensatory education students are admitted as members of the Freshman Year Alternative Program. Once students have successfully completed 40 quarter hours with a 2.0 quality point average they may transfer to one of the Basic Colleges — Liberal Arts, Education, Criminal Justice, Business Administration, etc. — with full transfer of credits. They can still complete their B.S. or B.A. program in five (5) years as do all other University students.

This site was selected on the following bases: (1) The college program is geared specifically for compensatory education students, (2) The college was willing to cooperate in this study, as the Dean is desirous of ascertaining whether a life planning or life planning/counseling program will assist in the retention of students.

2. Classroom Settings

Treatments for the experimental groups, group counseling sessions, and testing for all subjects will be conducted in the life planning classrooms. Classrooms at Northeastern University to be utilized will be almost identical: each is approximately 32 feet by 22 feet or 704 square feet (65.4 square meters). Each classroom is equipped in a similar fashion with green slate blackboards covering one wall, windows on another wall, and bulletin boards on the other two. About 30 portable seats with attached writing arms occupy each room. Standards for modern university classrooms will be in effect. The individual counseling aspects will take place in a conference room at the University designed for this purpose.

3. Subjects

The subjects for this experiment will consist of approximately seventy-five freshmen enrolled in compensatory education writing courses at University College. They will be drawn at random from the total population of approximately 200 compensatory education students and assigned to one of three treatment groups.

It is expected that the subjects will range in age from eighteen years to twenty-three years with eighteen the modal age. It is estimated that the students will have a mean Verbal Scholastic Aptitude Test score of approximately 380 and a mean Mathematics Scholastic Aptitude Test score of approximately 400. It is also estimated that the students will have had a mean rank in the third fifth (quintile) of their secondary school graduating class. Actual data on age and past academic achievement will be reported in the dissertation.

4. Procedures for Protection of Human Subjects

The Life Planning Course is required for University College compensatory education students; therefore, all students will have an opportunity to participate in this course during their freshman year and will not be excluded because of assignment to the control group in this experiment. Students will be informed that their test results will be used to help evaluate the course and they will be asked to sign a consent form giving permission to use information from their files. Students will be assured that individual test results will not be used and that only group data will be reported.

5. *Treatments*

Beginning in the Fall of 1979, every compensatory education student is required to complete, during the freshman year, a two credit course entitled 90.311 Life Planning. This course is the major treatment of this investigation (Treatment₁) and is described below. The entire curriculum is contained in Appendix C. In addition to Treatment₁ (Life Planning), a second treatment will consist of a combination of Life Planning and Career Counseling (Treatment₂), described below. The activities are described in Appendix D. A third treatment group will not receive the treatment during the first quarter but will be enrolled in 90.311 later in the academic year. The academic programs and the academic faculty for the three groups (Treatment₁, Treatment₂, and No Treatment) will otherwise be identical.

Treatment₁: Life Planning Course No. 90.311
As An Independent Variable (T₁)

The Life Planning course is a two quarter hour credit course. It meets for two hours per week for twelve (12) weeks for a total of twenty-four hours of treatment. The maximum enrollment per section is twenty-five students.

Life Planning curriculum consists of the following topics: Introduction to the Course, Introduction to Co-operative Education, Career Information, Self-Assessment, Resume Writing, Decision Making, Goal Setting, Problem Solving, the Interview.*

Treatment₂: Life Planning Course and Career Counseling
As An Independent Variable (T₂)

The group randomly assigned to Treatment₂ will complete the Life Planning Course curriculum. In addition, they will receive one quarter hour of credit for completing a Career Counseling Program. This program will consist of 10 one-hour

---

*NOTE: For economy, several pages have been omitted here. Complete details of Treatment ₁ are contained in the Appendices of the proposal.

sessions (8 group sessions and 2 individual sessions).

A. Group Career Counseling Sessions

Materials for the group career counseling treatment (T_2) have been taken from the College Entrance Examination Board's *Decisions and Outcomes* program designed to assist college students and adults who are faced with educational or career decisions. The College Entrance Examination Board is a non-profit organization that provides tests and other educational services for students, schools, and colleges.

Exercises and activities in *Decisions and Outcomes* were field tested with adults in 1973. *Decisions and Outcomes* deals with typical and real-life situations faced by many young adults in a variety of settings and situations. The exercises provide participants with an opportunity to learn more about themselves and their peers.

This aspect of the treatment includes exercises that emphasize the contingency relationship between behavior and outcome and exercises that raise expectations of achieving objectives. The entire program is described in Appendix D.

Treatment by Sessions

Session 1: Relative Importance of Decisions

This session focuses on categorizing decisions according to their perceived importance. The exercises provide a natural lead-in to locus of control internal-external orientation (see Appendix D).

Session 2: Clarifying Values for Sound Decision Making

The utilization of a passage from *Alice in Wonderland* illustrates that being clear about what one wants is important in sound decision making. The exercise gives practice in clarifying values and goals (see Appendix D).

Session 3: Consequences of Decision Making

Students will be asked to read a passage describing a day in the life of a seventeen-year-old student who makes seventeen decisions in the course of a day. Students will rank them in order of importance and discuss the *consequences* of each decision.

Social Learning Theory (Rotter, 1975) states that locus of control orientation is related to the value that a person places on a goal. The exercises involve looking at career objectives through skillful decision making and by clarifying values. It is assumed that an individual's desire to formulate career objectives will be of high value. In addition, the exercises foster goal-setting, which can be assumed to raise an individual's expectancy of achieving the goal. Exercises emphasize the contingency relationship between behavior and outcome; therefore, Sessions 1-3 should assist in modifying locus of control orientation toward increased internality and also lead to greater career maturity.

Session 4: Establishing Goals

This activity (see Appendix D) emphasizes the need for young adults to plan for a career by understanding and clarifying their own values and objectives. Students are asked to outline clear career objectives based on personal values.

Session 5: Predicting Outcomes

It is important to think about possible consequences of each alternative action that a person may contemplate. Students are asked to predict outcomes from contemplated actions regarding career choice (see Appendix D).

Individuals should place value on these activities, and expectancies of achieving goals should be raised. The exercises also emphasize the contingency relationship between behavior and outcome; thus, Sessions 4-5 should assist in modifying locus of control orientation and also heighten career maturity.

Sessions 6-8: Case Studies — Decision Making and Problem Solving

Three critical decisions to be made are presented. Values, goals, risk taking, and possible outcomes are discussed in conjunction with the cases (see Appendix D).

These exercises should also heighten expectations that behavior, guided by decision-making/problem-solving principles, will lead to desired goals. Sessions 6-8 should contribute to locus of control modification and increased career maturity by reinforcing perception of the contingency relationship between behavior and reinforcement.

B. Individual Career Counseling

During the term, two individual career counseling sessions will be held for each subject involved in Treatment$_2$ to discuss aspects of the life planning course and the group career counseling component in personal conference.

Locus of Control Change Techniques to Be Used in the Career Counseling Component

There are numerous procedures and suggestions contained in the works of MacDonald, 1972; Gardner and Beatty, 1980; Gardner and Gardner, 1974; Gardner and Warren, 1978; Reimanis and Schaefer, 1974 on how to modify locus of control on an individual or group basis. These techniques have been supported by numerous studies (see Review of the Literature). The career counselor will apply these techniques in both the individual and group sessions where applicable and logical. The following are some examples of these procedures:

A. As examples, use of the words *it, you,* or *one* places responsibility for behavior outside of the self in contrast to the more personal pronoun *I.*

B. Challenging or confronting external statements (e.g., "they want me to be . . .") with internal retorts (e.g., "what do *you* want to do?").

C. Rewording internal statements (e.g., "I'll search out career information").

D. Other examples would include the change from *but* to *and* and *can't* to *won't.* "I'd like to apply for that position, but I'm frightened, and I can't" to "I'd like to apply for the position, and I'm frightened, and I won't".

Subjects will be asked to recognize and focus upon the contingencies of their behavior. If they do such and such, then such and such will occur. They will be questioned as to what they could have done differently to change outcomes of past and present problems and what they could do in the future to cope with career problems.

Such verbal strategies have been found to be empirically effective in modifying locus of control in the direction of internality (Dua, 1970; Felton and Biggs, 1972, 1973; Majumder, Greever, Holt, and Friedland, 1973; Reimanis, 1974).

6. No Treatment Group (*T₀*)

The control group will be comprised of twenty-five (25) students assigned at random who will have the same academic program as the treatment group but will not be enrolled in the Life Planning Course nor receive the Life Planning Course/Counseling component during the fall quarter.

7. Dependent Variables

There are two dependent variables. The first, locus of control of reinforcement, will be determined by the Different Situations Inventory, Self-Report Form.

The second dependent variable, career maturity, will be determined by the Crites Career Maturity Inventory, Competence Test, Parts 3, 4, and 5.

8. Faculty

All other academic courses in which the two treatment groups and the control group are enrolled will be taught by the same professors.

Both Life Planning treatment groups will be taught by the same professor with that same person, trained as a counselor, also providing the Career Counseling component.

9. Materials and Presentation Format

As part of the Life Planning program, students will utilize the basic text *Working* by Studs Terkel, published by Avon Books, New York, 1975 and *Career Planning Student Workbook* by Karen E. McGuire and Jane S. Schachter, Northeastern University Press, 1978. The syllabus for the course appears in Appendix C.

Those subjects involved in T_2 — the Life Planning course/Career Counseling component — will utilize the case studies and exercises that appear in Appendix D.

10. Experimental Design

This study will use as a basic model a true experimental approach: Design 6: The Post-Test Only Control Group De-

$$
\begin{array}{ll}
R \quad X_a & O_1 \\[2mm]
R \quad X_b & O_2 \\[2mm]
R & O_3
\end{array}
$$

Figure 2. Experimental Design. Reprinted from D. T. Campbell and J. C. Stanley. *Experimental and Quasi-experimental designs for research* (Chicago, Rand McNally, 1963), with permission of the publisher.

sign (Campbell and Stanley, 1963, p. 25).

This true experimental design (Fig. 2) has the advantage of avoiding possible effects of testing and is a much underutilized design (Campbell and Stanley, page 25). It controls for internal validity (history, maturation, testing, instrumentation, regression, selection, mortality, and interaction) and for the interaction of testing and treatment (external validity) (Campbell and Stanley, p. 8).

11. Instrumentation

A. Different Situations Inventory (Appendix E)

The Different Situations Inventory (DSI), developed by Gardner and Warren (1978) is a locus of control measure which consists of two (2) separate scales: a self-report instrument and a rating scale to be completed by a person familiar with some of the attitudinal and behavioral characteristics of the person being rated.

This investigator will utilize the Self-Report Form, a 20 question paper and pencil test of forced choices scored in the direction of internality.

1. Reliability

In 1978, Ifenwanta reported a test-retest reliability coefficient of .90. An item analysis revealed the test to be "a very reliable instrument with about 85 percent of the test items significantly correlated to the total score." Ifenwanta also reported that the Different Situations Inventory, Self-Report Form was "strongly discriminative between the upper and lower median groups" (Ifenwanta, 1978, pp. 52-53).

2. Validity

Ifenwanta (1978) reports a high, significant correlation between the DSI, Self-Report Form, and Rotter's I-E scale (r = .66, p = .01). The rating form correlates significantly with the Nowicki-Strickland Locus of Control Scale (Wilton, 1978), the James Locus of Control Scale, and Rotter's I-E Scale (Von Esch, 1978). Wilton reports an internal consistency coefficient of .856 for the rating form. Both the rating form and the self-report form have identical items.

In addition to criterion related validity on both forms, there are several studies indicating good construct validity. One would predict from social learning theory that persons with an internal locus of control would be more likely to exhibit higher levels of career maturity. As predicted, a number of studies with various populations ranging from Nigerian adults to middle school American children to college women and others found significant correlations between both forms of the DSI and the various measures of career maturity developed by Crites (see Bigelow, 1980; Cowan, 1979; Grossman, 1979; Ifenwanta, 1978; and Wilton, 1978).

Another test of construct validity is the study of the relationship between locus of control and achievement. One would predict a significant relationship between achievement and locus of control. Very little work has been done in this area with the DSI, but those studies that have been done are consistent with theory and similar work on other locus of control scales. Von Esch (1978) found that the rating form of the DSI discriminated between high and low achievers in a CETA training program. He also reports an unpublished study by Gardner and Kurtz in which they found a significant correlation between the self-report form of the DSI and grade point average of female college students (N=66).

Finally, a number of theorists on locus of control change-techniques (e.g., MacDonald, 1972; Gardner and Gardner, 1974; Gardner and Warren, 1978; Gardner and Beatty, 1980) suggest that certain theoretically based procedures can change a person's locus of control orientation through counseling and/or instructional strategies. Two studies, applying these theoretically based treatments using the self-report form of the DSI, report significant increases in "internality" on the part of those subjects receiving such change-technique treatments (Beatty and Gardner, 1979; Bigelow, 1980).

The issue of content or face validity was addressed during the development of the scale. The original items were submitted to three judges who had published research on locus of control. Each judge was asked to label the answer to each item as "external" or "internal." The three judges were in 100 percent agreement with each other and with the authors on every item.

In summary, the Different Situations Inventory is still in the experimental stage. However, the scale possesses strong evidence of good reliability and excellent content, criterion-related and construct validity. It was, therefore, determined to be an appropriate instrument for this study.

B. Career Maturity Inventory (CMI) (Appendix F)

The result of efforts to develop a heuristic model for career development research purposes, the Crites Inventory is based on the concept postulated by Ginzberg, Ginsburg, Alexrad, and Herma (1951) that ". . . the choice of an occupation is a process, not simply a one time event which . . . progresses through differentiable periods of deliberation culminating in a more or less satisfactory and satisfying compromise between personal needs and occupational realities."

Crites constructed the CMI to measure two components of his conception of the career choice process: (1) career choice attitudes (comprised of five variables — decisiveness, involvement, independence, orientation, and compromise) and (2) career choice competencies (comprised of five variables — self-appraisal, occupational information, goal selection, planning, and problem solving). Thus, the Inventory has two parts: an Attitude Scale (one test) and a Competence Test (five subtests). Each of these six tests yields a discrete score.

Wilton (1978) conducted a factor analysis procedure to determine whether a composite (factor) score of career maturity could be obtained from the discrete scores available on the individual sections of the test and found that "the career maturity scores loaded on one factor, an indication that they represented one overall dimension or factor of career maturity" (p. 38). Unfortunately, one subtest, Part 5, Problem Solving, was not included in the study because of time constraints in the testing sequence.

This present study will be concerned with measures of career maturity as defined in Parts 3, 4, 5 of the Competence Tests. The Competence Test was constructed to assess "what might be designated as comprehension and problem-solving abilities as they pertain to the vocational choice process" (Crites, 1973, p. 9). Part 3, Choosing A Job (Goal Selection), "can be called the true reasoning" process of career decision making and can be regarded as "one of the hallmarks of maturity" (Crites, 1973, p. 25). The Goal Selection subtest (Part 3) was "developed to assess the ability to relate self to work" (Crites, 1973, p. 27).

Part 4, Looking Ahead (Planning), represents the next logical step in career decision making. With a goal selected, Part 4 attempts to measure the planning element of how the goal is to be achieved. In 1960, Super and Overstreet, as reported by Crites, found that the "single most significant factor among the various indices of vocational maturity was planning" (Crites, 1973, p. 27).

According to Crites, Part 5 of the Competence Test — What Should They Do? — was constructed to measure "how well an individual can solve the problems occurring in the career developmental tasks that one is expected to accomplish in preparation for entry into the world of work" (Crites, 1978, p. 28).

1. Reliability

Reliability of the Competence Test is demonstrated by internal consistency coefficients which range from .72 to .90 with only two exceptions. Internal consistency figures for Parts 3 and 4 are both reported to be .90 with older adolescents.

2. Validity

Content validity is assured from a combination of two factors: (1) the subject matter of the items was drawn from actual career counseling interviews with high school and college students and (2) the subtests were conceived specifically to define and measure a particular cognitive aspect of career maturity, for example, problem solving.

Validity measures of the Competence Test were begun in 1975, and data reported to the developers has seemed to confirm theoretical expectancies, models, and constructs. Studies on the construct validity have found that in most grades the Occupational Information, Goal Selection, and Planning subtests appear to have the highest intercorrelation, .60, and all intercorrelations are significant at or beyond the .01 level (Crites, 1973, pp. 30-35).

12. Procedures

Assignment to Control and Treatment Groups

Random assignment of subjects to the two treatments and the control group will be made.

All freshman compensatory education students enrolling in University College of Northeastern University constitute the population and have an equal possibility of being chosen for treatment groups.

13. Administration of Instruments

Both the Self-Report Form of the Different Situations Inventory (Gardner and Warren, 1978) and Parts 3, 4, and 5 of the Competence Test of the Career Maturity Inventory (Crites, 1973) will be administered on a post-treatment basis to the two experimental groups and the control group on the same day.

During the final class session, all three groups will be administered the Different Situations Inventory Self-Report Form and Parts, 3, 4, 5 of the Competence Test of the Career Maturity Inventory.

All tests will be given by the regular teachers in order to avoid "experimenter" and "Hawthorne" effects in test scores (Isaac and Michael, 1971, pp. 60-63). The teacher will be trained by the investigator in methods of test administration. The investigator will supervise the testing procedures, but outside of the classroom.

14. Timing

The Life Planning course (Treatment$_1$) and the Life Planning course plus counseling (Treatment$_2$) will be offered during the fall quarter 1979 if permission is granted to proceed.

SAMPLE 15

"Methodology" section from an alumni follow-up study.

Subjects

Subjects will all be graduates of the Bachelor of Science degree program in the Special Education Department of the School of Education for 1976 (January, May, September), 1977 (January, May, September), and 1978 (January, May). Alumni from the Special Education Department will be selected for study on the following bases: (a) the Special Education Department has the largest enrollment of Bachelor of Science students within the School of Education (approximately 40%), (b) students majoring in Special Education complete a greater percentage of their total academic work within the School of Education compared to other undergraduate majors, (c) the department strongly supports the study, and (d) Special Education positions are thought to be more readily available than other education positions at this time, because of U.S. Public Law 94-142.

The subjects for this ex post facto study will consist of 316 graduates from the official graduation lists of the Bachelor of Science in Special Education program who graduated from the School of Education, Boston University, within the past three years (1976, 1977, 1978). The sampling frame consists of the commencement lists for the graduation dates shown in Figure 3.

Sample Size

Questionnaires will be mailed to the entire population (male and female) of the three years (1976, 1977, 1978) in order to ensure that at least 100 questionnaires will be returned for evaluation. According to Parten (1966): "One procedure for determining the minimum number of classes into which to break down a base figure is to divide the base number by the proposed number of categories. The resulting figure should not be lower than 10" (p. 298).

Graduation Date	Number Graduated
January, 1976 May, 1976 September, 1976	113*
January, 1977 May, 1977 September, 1977	130
January, 1978 May, 1978 September, 1978**	73***
TOTAL	316

* One student deleted due to overseas address
** One student deleted due to overseas address
*** September, 1978 graduates not included in study

Figure 3. Official Graduation Statistics for 1976, 1977, and 1978 Special Education Students.

Procedures for Protection of Human Subjects

Subjects for this study will be forwarded a consent form which will ask them to sign an agreement to participate in the study. Subjects will be informed that the collected data will be used in a dissertation, with individuals remaining anonymous and only group data being reported. (See Appendix A for copy of consent agreement.)

Procedures

This study will primarily be concerned with determining which of the six selected variables, if any, will be significantly correlated to employment in the field of special education. Each variable was selected on the basis of findings from previous studies of employment patterns (see Chapter Two and Review of the Literature) and/or clinical judgement. For instance, numerous studies indicate that grade point average is significantly related to employment in various fields (e.g.,

Hakel & Mannel, 1969). Thus this variable is hypothesized to be an important factor. Conversely, there is apparently very little information on the relationship between Scholastic Achievement Test scores and subsequent employment. Yet it seems probable, on a common sense basis, other factors being equal, that Scholastic Achievement Test scores may be considered by administrators when hiring personnel. Thus this variable was selected.

The six predictor variables are as follows:

1. Total grade point average
2. Grade point average in professional courses
3. Boston University Placement File
   a. Establishment of a placement file
   b. Forwarding of the placement file to prospective employers
4. Scholastic Achievement Verbal Test score
5. Scholastic Achievement Mathematics Test score
6. Total Scholastic Achievement Test score — verbal plus mathematics.

Questionnaire Survey

Rationale

To obtain data deemed *essential to the study, but not available from existing records* maintained at the school, a questionnaire will be designed. The main advantage of the mailed questionnaire procedure is that it is generally *faster* and *less expensive* than other methods. (Moser, 1961; Parten, 1966)

Moreover, Parten (1966) points out that —

1. the questionnaire may reach individuals who are not otherwise accessible to investigators.
2. antagonism to investigators is avoided.
3. questions are standardized.
4. questionnaires can be returned at the convenience of the respondent.
5. persons who are widely scattered may be easier to locate by mail.

However, these advantages may be offset by some serious drawbacks (Parten, 1966). These include the fact that people who return the questionnaires may not be representative of the ones to whom the questionnaires are mailed and the return rate may be low. Despite these and other disadvantages, the author will use a written questionnaire data collection procedure. This procedure is more feasible for the purposes of this study than such techniques as personal interviews, group interviews, and telephone interviews. There are specific strategies shown to be effective in counteracting the major problems inherent in questionnaires. These strategies will be incorporated in the study design and the mailing and follow-up procedures related to the questionnaire phase of this study. They are described below.

Questionnaire Design

A review of the literature concerning the use of questionnaires reveals that response rates can range from 10 to 90 percent. According to Moser (1961, p. 179) "If the sample is of the general population, rather than of a special group, strenuous efforts are usually needed to bring the response rate above about 30 to 40 percent." In addition, most authorities agree that a certain proportion of nonrespondence cannot be prevented. According to Parten (1966) major factors that tend to reduce rates are:

> (1) the characteristics such as sex, economic status, and educational level of the groups solicited; (2) the interest in the subject of the investigation; (3) the prestige of the sponsoring groups among the recipients of the questionnaire; and (4) strong agreement or disagreement with the propositions about which they are surveyed, are all related to the proportion of replies obtained (p. 391).

With respect to possible respondent differences (as they affect response rate) on sex, economic status and educational level, the subjects of this study will be relatively homogeneous on these variables. All subjects will hold a Bachelors degree from the same program in the same private university. Data on parent occupation and income for students at the university indicate that their social economic status is middle class, the majority being upper middle class.

Another important factor affecting response rates is the "interests" of the group being studied in the sponsoring organization and in the topic under consideration (Parten, 1966). Since all subjects surveyed were trained as "special educators," interest in the topic will be assumed. Moreover, interest in the sponsoring agency, their alma mater, will also be assumed. In addition, a cover letter endorsing the study, signed by the Dean of the School of Education, Boston University, will be included with the mailing packet. Parten (1966) states that endorsements signed by prominent individuals add prestige and creditability to a questionnaire survey and may increase return rate.

In order to enhance further the return rate, the following procedures will be incorporated into the design of the questionnaire:

1. *Number of Questions:* The number of questions selected will be kept to an absolute minimum. Only data that are not available from records will be collected. Several authorities on survey design (e.g. Parten, 1966; Moser, 1961) point out that the shorter the questionnaire, the higher the return rate.

2. *Wording of Questions:* According to Parten (1966), Best (1977), Moser (1961) and others, simple, easy to understand questions increase the return rate. Therefore, one of the major design goals will be to simplify the wording of the questions. Any "questionable word" will be checked against Payne's (1963) list of "1000 Frequent Familiar Words" and alternate words considered for those that might be misunderstood. In addition, care will be taken in the formulation of the questions to ensure that they will secure the information desired. Catch words or jargon will be screened out. Since the questions are aimed at obtaining factual as opposed to opinion information, a simple dichotomous or completion format will be used.

Appendix B will provide an analysis of each question contained in the survey including the following:

1. question type (e.g., dichotomous, completion).
2. subjects to whom the questions are directed.
3. hypothesis related to the question.
4. data collection code for each question.

3. *Pilot Testing of Questionnaires:* The final draft version of

the questionnaire will be pilot tested on a small group of School of Education (practicing teachers) graduate students. The purpose of the pilot study will be to determine test-retest reliability (stability, one-week interval) and to gain feedback on possible ambiguities of items. After the second administration, the pilot group will be asked to offer suggestions for improving clarity.

Once these suggestions are integrated, the questionnaire will be professionally printed.

4. *Questionnaire Format:* Several formats proposed by different authorities were reviewed. The contingency format suggested by Babbie (1973) was selected as most appropriate for this study. According to Babbie (1973) the proper use of contingency questions can facilitate the respondents task in answering the questionnaire and can also improve the quality of the data produced.

The *CONTINGENCY FORMAT:*

   a. reduces the amount of time required to complete the questionnaire.

   b. provides a neat and eye appealing format.

These are important factors influencing return rate.

The contingency format also has the advantage of providing a "road map" to the next appropriate question and facilitates the tabulation of the data.

5. *Appearance:* Most authorities agree that the appearance of the questionnaire is of utmost importance in terms of response rate. Ideally, a professionally printed questionnaire is most effective in increasing response rate (Babbie, 1973). It also offers other advantages:

   a. offers the option of reducing the type size which in turn reduces the *overall size* of the questionnaire.

   b. offers the possibility of using boldface type to *emphasize key words* or phrases in a question.

   c. permits use of a *one-page* questionnaire.

6. *Color:* Parten (1966) points out that in certain marketing studies yellow paper (of all colors used) had the *highest percentage of returns.* Accordingly, a high quality 8 1/2″ × 11″ yellow textured bond paper will be used for the questionnaire

(see Appendix C).

7. *Timing:* Questionnaires for the first mailing will be sent on a Wednesday afternoon (March 8th) so that they will be delivered to the subjects on a Friday or Saturday morning; there is *considerable evidence to show* that most questionnaires tend to be filled out during the weekend. Questionnaires that arrive early in the week tend to be laid aside and usually result in lower return rates (Parten, 1966).

According to Parten (1966, p. 386) "New stamps or commemorative stamps affect results if used immediately after their issue, when they are still a novelty." The Einstein Commemorative stamp that will be issued to the public on March 6th, 1979, will be used on both the mailing and return address envelopes included in the questionnaire packet.

8. *Mailing and Return Envelopes:* A white commercial size (4 1/2" × 10 1/4") envelope will be utilized for mailing the questionnaire, letter of endorsement, permission statement, and return addressed envelope. The return, self-addressed envelope will be standard size (4 1/4" × 9 1/2"), yellow in color, with a printed return address (see Appendix D).

9. *Mailing Addressses:* A machine listing of 1976, 1977, and 1978 Bachelor of Science Special Education majors will be obtained from the Boston University Alumni Office. This list will be compared to the official commencement lists with appropriate additions being made to insure all graduates are included. Graduates with foreign addresses will be deleted from the mailing list. To encourage responses, all envelopes will be hand addressed. Both the mailing and return envelopes will have "PERSONAL AND CONFIDENTIAL" printed in the lower left corner (see Appendix D).

10. *Official Endorsement:* A review of the literature (e.g., Parten, 1966; Moser, 1961) shows that official endorsement or sponsorship of the study enhances the response rate. Sponsorship for the study was obtained from the Dean of the School of Education, Boston University. An endorsement signed by the Dean will therefore be included (see Appendix E).

11. *Incentive:* Most authorities (Parten, 1966; Moser, 1961; Babbie, 1973; et al.) state that incentives to the responder can increase response rate. Incentives such as money and prizes

were considered and ruled out for this study due to possible violation of state and federal laws concerning lotteries and the possibility of "coercion" in use of human subjects in research. Subjects in the study will be offered an *abstract of the completed study* in Newsletter format (see Appendix E). Since all subjects are professionals, or received their Bachelor of Science degrees in the same professional field, and all are from the same program (which has a high cohesion of skills), it is therefore assumed that the offer of an abstract will enhance the response rate.

Follow-up Procedures on Non-Respondents

The success or failure of a mail survey rests on the return of the questionnaires by the respondents. If the questionnaire is properly designed, printed, packaged, and mailed at the appropriate time, the next procedure for insuring a high percentage of returns is a planned follow-up mailing. Parten (1966) advocates the use of smaller samples with follow-up letters rather than larger samples without reminders. Parten further states that the greater the number of follow-up letters, the higher the proportion of returns that may be expected, within certain limits of course.

The follow-up procedures used in this study will be based on a model by Galfo and Miller (1970). This model is a three-cycle plan with the first cycle consisting of the initial mailing of the questionnaire followed by a tabulation of data with a percent computation on returns. The second cycle consists of a follow-up by mail to non-respondents with a new deadline, which is followed by a tabulation of data and percent of returns kept separate from a first return. The third cycle consists of a mail or telephone follow-up with tabulation of data and a percent computation of responses (see Appendix F).

First Follow-up

The complete package will be mailed to non-respondents with an accompanying reminder note (see Appendix G). Einstein Commemorative stamps will be used again. A specific return date of March 30th will be hand written on the reminder memo.

Second Follow-up

The second follow-up will be a telephone survey to a random sample of 15 non-respondents. Phone calls will be made in the early evening, which is hypothesized to be the best time of day to reach the non-respondents. Subjects will be encouraged to respond to the telephone interview and asked to mail permission forms immediately.

Control of Bias

The major independent variable in the questionnaire will be employment status in the field of special education. Percentages of yes and no responses to this key question about employment status will be maintained by mailing cycle.

A planned review of the non-response/response pattern to this item will be used to test for bias in responses. This procedure for checking response bias is based on the assumption that the proportion of yes-no responses to the employment status item should be consistent for each cycle.

Chapter 10

SAMPLE DATA ANALYSIS PROCEDURES FOR EXPERIMENTAL, QUASI-EXPERIMENTAL, AND FOLLOW-UP SURVEY PROPOSALS

SAMPLE 16

"DATA Analysis" section from a true experimental design proposal. *

Data Analysis

The major purposes of this study are as follows: (1) to investigate the general experimental effects of teaching life planning

---

*The data analysis section of the dissertation proposal is a key section that many doctoral candidates find difficult to write. Yet, if the "design" is crystal clear, especially if one uses designs recommended by experts (e.g. Campbell and Stanely, 1963; Cook and Campbell, 1979), the appropriate statistical procedures are usually self-evident. To reiterate our earlier suggestions, if you are having difficulty with writing the Data Analysis section, take another course in design/statistics and/or hire a tutor. However, be careful when hiring a tutor. To borrow from Robert Townsend's comments about computers and computer experts:

STATISTICIANS, COMPUTERS AND THEIR PRIESTS
First, get through your head that computers are big, expensive, fast, dumb adding machine-typewriters. Then realize that most of the computer technicians and statistician-tutors, for hire to graduate students, are complicators, not simplifiers. They're trying to make it look tough. Not easy. They're building a mystique, a priesthood, their own mumbo-jumbo ritual to keep you from knowing what they — and you — are doing.

When (if) you employ a "hired gun," make darn certain he/she *helps you learn* how to select and defend the best statistical procedures for your study. Insist on tutoring and consulting in the King's English. Don't let this "priest" put you down! It's your hard earned money. Get your money's worth. There isn't any qualified doctoral candidate who can't learn the basic lingo of computers and statistics given the right training.

Study Examples 16, 17, and 18 carefully. Make sure you know what you're talking about when your turn comes because you will have to defend your data analysis procedures by *yourself.*

curriculum on career maturity, (2) to investigate the differences between a life planning course treatment and a life planning course with a career counseling component emphasizing change techniques on career maturity, (3) to investigate the general experimental effects of teaching life planning curriculum on locus of control orientation, and (4) to investigate the differences between a life planning course treatment and a life planning course with a career counseling component emphasizing change techniques on locus of control orientation.

These questions will be tested in the context of the compensatory education classes currently being conducted at Northeastern University. Treatments will consist of (1) a life planning course as defined in *Methodology* pages 26-29, (2) the life planning course combined with a career counseling component as defined in *Methodology* pages 29-34, and (3) no treatment.

The basic design for this proposed study is a true experimental design, the Randomized Post-Test Only Control Group Design (Campbell and Stanley, 1963, p. 25). This design permits a direct determination of the main effects of treatment on the four dependent variables: locus of control as measured by the Different Situations Inventory and career maturity as measured by three separate subtests of the Crites Career Maturity Inventory, Competence Tests 3, 4, and 5.

Orthogonal comparisons will be made to test for the general experimental effects of the life planning treatment (Hypotheses 1 and 4). Orthogonal comparisons will also be made to test for differences between the two experimental treatments (Hypotheses 2 and 5).

In order to test Hypothesis 4, which is concerned with the correlations between locus of control and three subtests of the Career Maturity Inventory, three Pearson product-moment coefficients of correlation will be computed.

SAMPLE 17

"Data Analysis" section from an alumni follow-up study proposal.

1. Means and standard deviations for all subgroups and the total group will be reported in tabular form for all variables.

2. Estimates of the relationship between employment in special education and total Scholastic Achievement Test scores, Scholastic Achievement Verbal Test scores, Scholastic Achievement Mathematics Test scores, total grade point average and grade point average in professional courses (Hypotheses 1-5) will be made using the point biserial coefficient of correlation. (Note: the point biserial procedure is used when one variable is continuous and the other dichotomous) (Roscoe, 1975, p. 113).

3. To estimate the relationship between employment in special education and the establishment of a placement file (Hypothesis 6), the tetrachoric coefficient of correlation will be used. (Note: the tetrachoric correlation coefficient is numerically equivalent to the Pearson r and is used to estimate the correlation between two dichotomous variables) (Guilford, 1965).

4. To test for differences between and among groups where such meaningful comparisons will be helpful in interpreting the major findings and in describing various subgroups, analysis of variance, *t* tests and chi square will be employed as appropriate.

SAMPLE 18

"Data Analysis" section from a quasi-experimental design study.

The main purposes of this study are (1) to investigate the relationship of resume writing and career maturity, (2) to investigate the relationship of goal setting to resume writing performance and career maturity, (3) to investigate the generalization of goal setting behavior to a professionally related task outside of the experimental setting, and (4) to investigate the relationship of locus of control to career maturity and task performance.

The above questions will be tested in the context of a resume writing class conducted in a two-year college in the Metropolitan Boston area with sophomore women enrolled in a business program. The treatments will consist of standard resume writing instruction (as defined in Methodology, pp. 24 to 26), resume writing instruction with a goal-setting emphasis (as defined in Methodology, pp. 26 to 27), and no treatment.

The basic data analysis design for this study will be a 3 × 2 factorial analysis of covariance, Table I, which will permit a direct determination of the main effects of treatment × locus of control orientation as well as their interaction (Kerlinger, 1973, pp. 242-270).

There are three dependent variables, each of which will be

TABLE I

SCHEMATIC REPRESENTATION OF
THE 3 × 2 EXPERIMENTAL DESIGN

		Standard Resume Writing	Goal Setting Emphasis	No Treatment
L O C U S	Internal	ILC/SRW	ILC/GSE	ILC/NT
O F C O N T R O L	External	ELC/SRW	ELC/GSE	ELC/NT

ILC = Internal Locus of Control
ELC = External Locus of Control
SRW = Standard Resume Writing
GSE = Goal-Setting Emphasis
NT = No Treatment

used to test various hypotheses concerned with the main effects. The three dependent variables are career maturity (Crites Career Maturity Inventory, Competence Tests 3 and 4), typing performance (average scores on timed writings) and resume writing performance (as rated by a panel of experts).

In order to test the hypotheses concerned with the effects of the treatment on two measures of career maturity and its differential effects on two classifications of locus of control orientation, four Two-Way Analyses of Covariance (COVAR) will be employed. Since it will not be possible to randomly assign subjects to treatments, Two-Way COVAR has been selected as the best method for controlling for possible treatment group differences in career maturity prior to treatment. The covariate will be the pre-treatment career maturity measures on Competence Tests 3 and 4.

According to Roscoe (1969) "The analysis of covariance . . . permits *statistical* rather than *experimental* control of variables. The result is equivalent to matching the various experimental groups with respect to the variable or variables being controlled" (p. 351).

The use of the initial career maturity score as the covariate is further supported by Roscoe: "The use of analysis of covariance ordinarily involves a pretest (the variable to be controlled) and a posttest (the criterion). . . . In some circumstances, it may be completely appropriate to use the same instrument for both pretest and posttest" (p. 352).

Further testing of Hypotheses 1 and 2 can be made *a priori* according to Kimmel (1970): "There is nothing to prevent an experimenter from making a particular comparison which is implied a priori by his analysis of the problem, so long as his statistical test allows for all possible comparisons that could be made in relation to the same experimental hypothesis" (p. 160).

Dunnet's *t* is recommended by Roscoe (1975) as an appropriate a priori procedure for "comparing a control group to two or more experimental groups (p. 311). A Dunnet's *t* will be used to compare the mean scores of the combined resume writing groups to the mean score of the no-treatment group to determine the differences in treatment versus no treatment (Hypothesis 1).

In order to test the hypotheses about the transfer of goal setting behavior to a professionally-related task outside of the experimental setting, a quasi-experimental Multiple Time-Series Design for nonequivalent groups (Campbell and Stanley, 1963, p. 55) will be used. Analysis of variance with repeated measures will be used to test for main effects.

The pre- and posttreatment time series design offers several advantages according to Campbell and Stanley (1963): "This design . . . gains in certainty of interpretation from the multiple measures plotted, as the experimental effect is in a sense twice demonstrated, once against the control and once against the pre-X values in its own series" (p. 55).

The third dependent variable is resume writing performance, as rated by four judges (see Methodology of this proposal, pp. 30-32, for a detailed explanation of the procedures for the determination of resume quality, judges, etc.). To test the hypotheses concerned with resume writing performance, analysis of covariance will be employed. Subject's Freshman English grade will be used as the covariate to control for general (writing) ability in English. The grade is readily available in the students' files. Students will be asked to volunteer to allow access to their files as part of the "protection of human subject procedures" discussed previously in the methodology chapter.

Section III
How To Get Your Proposal Accepted

Expect to Succeed!

Chapter 11

SELLING IS NOT A FOUR-LETTER WORD

THE basic goal of the doctoral dissertation/ thesis proposal writer is to get the product accepted. This requires attention to all the factors and details that may enhance or deter the probabilities for acceptance. This means that you may need to sell your proposal to your committee. If "selling" yourself and your ideas seems painful to you, buy a book on how to sell. Better still, read books on taking charge of your life and being more assertive and confident. Remember, **only you can get that proposal accepted.** Some of the items you need to attend to in developing your sales campaign will be discussed in this chapter.

Committee Selection

All doctoral dissertation committees are made up of human beings living in the here and now. Many will have their own favorite TV show, some will even go to the movies, watch football, play with their children, and, except at doctoral hearings, are normal folks. As professionals, each member has his or her own agenda, biases, and interests.

Insist on your right as a "consumer" to have input into the selection of your doctoral committee. Work closely with your advisor in selecting a committee that is highly qualified. Highly successful and qualified people rarely have "insecure egos" that need to be fed by putting others down. The "tougher" your committee (meaning the more qualified) the "easier" it will be. First, they are capable of recognizing an "outstanding" proposal. On the other hand, they will have little patience with a poorly thought out proposal. If you have a good committee, they can make suggestions based on their own experience in doing research that can be very helpful to you.

Try to get a committee of persons *interested in your topic*. Interested people tend to be more cooperative and helpful. Don't pick a committee member because you had a course with him or her. That's nice, but you want a committee of highly qualified experts in your area of interest. Their interest in your topic may take several forms, by the way. They may not be doing research on exactly the same topic, for instance on anxiety, but they may be very interested in the population you have chosen, e.g. children, women, or entry-level managers, which means they will probably be interested in a study about anxiety in children, women, entry-level managers, etc.

If your department requires a bona fide statistician on your committee, please refer to our previous comments in the last chapter. Try to get a statistician who speaks English as opposed to statistics and who is, ideally, interested in your problem.

Try to select a committee made up of people who like each other. We know one very bright doctoral candidate who was held up for two years, despite an outstanding proposal, because two of his committee members were having a personal feud. If this happens to you, find out about the rules on "dumping" a committee member and don't be afraid to do so. It's *your* career that's at stake. Be quietly assertive of your rights as a student and as a human being. Remember that it is *your* money and time.

Read some of the current writings of your committee members. Not only will you find out what each member is interested in, you may learn something. It is always advisable to know a little about how a member thinks. An ounce of prevention is always worth a pound of cure.

An additional caveat about committee selection. Consider having one more person on your committee than the number required by your school. This ensures that you will still have the minimum required number if one member should be so inconsiderate as to die before your final hearing (it happens) or should accept another position halfway around the world. We're sure you've heard the old horror stories of candidates spending a fortune on long distance phone calls, plane tickets, etc., for a committee member who has left the university or gone on sabattical to Europe. Keep this in mind when you select your committee.

Aesthetics

Getting together an outstanding proposal usually starts with an OK from your advisor on the topic area. Your next step would be to write a short prospectus that would contain your problem statement, research questions, hypotheses, and a rough abstract of the design/methodology. If you think it advisable, get approval in writing by including a signature line at the bottom of the prospectus. Give your advisor two copies — one to sign and return to you and one to keep.

Don't hand in anything (even a draft) that isn't professional looking. Negative expectancies can kill you. Once someone has received junk from you they will expect the same quality next time. *Hire a professional typist.* This is no time to be cheap.

Assuming a favorable response to your prospectus, you are now ready to write your proposal. Unless you have an advisor who is willing to deal with you on a chapter-by-chapter basis, plan on handing in a complete, *professional* proposal. Continue with the professional typist. Don't photocopy with one of those second rate machines. Get it done on a good machine and on good paper. Have it *bound.* Velo binding looks professional and should cost under two dollars per copy. Type up a nice cover on colored stock. You can probably buy enough blank cover stock from an offset printing shop. Be fussy about the type style and format. If your department *expects* APA style, then give it to them in perfect form. Pay attention to headings, figures, tables, and illustrations. Proofread it yourself several times; then get someone who you know is a good proofreader to read it again. Do it well the first time and it will win you accolades. Besides, a "perfect" proposal is the first draft of your dissertation.

The Problem Hearing

Even though you have handed in an excellent proposal, you still need to face your committee in a formal hearing. We're not going to tell you not to be nervous because **everyone** is nervous at their own problem hearing. We *are* going to give you a few suggestions on how to control events, however.

One very effective technique we have suggested to our own students is the use of *overhead transparencies.* Having the key elements of your proposal on overheads means that you don't have to rely solely on your memory, and you can be sure that you won't forget any of the important points. If you visualize what happens when you use an overhead projector, you can see how it helps you to remain in control.

First, the room should be dim, but not necessarily dark, in order for everyone to see the screen. This prevents people from browsing through your proposal or their notes instead of listening to your presentation. Secondly, as soon as you turn on the projector and the screen is lit, all eyes automatically focus on the screen. This puts you on center stage and everyone is paying attention. Third, people don't usually interrupt a "performance," and that is exactly what you are giving. With the proper transparencies and a polished delivery, you will find that your committee members will probably wait until you have finished your presentation to ask their questions. If you have done a good job, they'll end up saying that you already answered the question they were going to ask. At one hearing using this approach, one of the committee members commented that she usually found hearings rather boring, but that she felt she actually learned something at this one.

The kinds of information you will want to have on overheads might include:

1. Quotes from the major theorist or theorists on whose work you are basing your proposal.
2. An outline of your statement of the problem.
3. Research questions.
4. Hypotheses.
5. Outline of the treatment, if appropriate.
6. Research design and data analysis procedures.

A useful feature of overheads is that you can make notes on the frame to help you remember important points. Your committee members can't see your notes, and you certainly look more professional when you're not shuffling index cards or papers. You will want to discuss some of your points without overheads. Remember to turn off the overhead light when you do this or people will still tend to look at the empty lighted screen.

If you don't know anything about overhead transparencies, go to the audio-visual or media department (or to the School of Education) and ask for some help. They are not difficult to make or to use.

Practice your presentation in front of people who will give you an unbiased reaction.

Likely Questions from Your Committee

Obviously you need to be able to justify your entire proposal, but there are specific items you should count on having to defend in your hearing.

1. WHY YOU SHOULD STUDY THIS SUBJECT. You can head off this question by discussing in the beginning of your presentation the importance of this topic to your field. You might want to mention how you became interested in the topic and why you feel the approach you have chosen is likely to be meaningful in the context of the theory. Then follow up with the overhead on theoretical support for your position.

2. RELIABILITY AND VALIDITY OF INSTRUMENTATION. The benefit of using validated instruments to measure your dependent variable is that the question of reliability and validity have been addressed by the test developer, and this information will be available from the publisher. Make sure you include this data in your proposal under the "Instrumentation" section. If you are planning on using a pilot instrument that does not have sufficient reliability and validity statistics, you should seriously consider using a second (validated) measure. This will give you a chance to contribute to data on the new instrument by correlating it with a similar measure. You will also avoid putting all your eggs in an untried basket. We don't recommend constructing a test for your doctoral dissertation, by the way; it takes years and a fair amount of money to do it properly.

3. LENGTH AND TYPE OF TREATMENT (OR SURVEY PROCEDURES). This is where the empirical support is useful. If you can say that treatments similar to yours have produced significant results in these specific cases and treatments of similar length have produced significant results in other cases, you can pretty well justify your selection of procedures and length of time. As we mentioned before, an overhead transparency showing an outline of the different treatments will make your discussion much clearer.

4. POPULATION. You probably won't have to justify the fact that you are going to study children, women, entry-level managers, etc. You may have to explain the selection process for the subjects in your study. Are you using random assignment? What does the original population look like? If you are not using random assignment, how are you selecting participants and how are you assigning treatments? Charts that graphically portray subject selection and assignment to treatment make good overheads.

5. RESEARCH DESIGN. If you are using a design mentioned in Campbell and Stanley as being acceptable for answering the questions you are posing, you're on safe ground. Nobody argues with Campbell and Stanley. You might want to illustrate your design on an overhead, which you can use when discussing its relative merits.

6. DATA ANALYSIS PROCEDURES. We've already made our views on this topic clear. If appropriate, it's helpful to illustrate your data analysis design in blocks, as shown in Table I, Sample 18, Chapter 10.

A sample table of contents from an actual dissertation follows on the next page. Tables of contents vary with the study and with individual school requirements, but this will give you a good idea of how yours might look.

One final message: **There is no Substitute for Hard Work.** To borrow from Thomas A. Edison:

> *Getting a Dissertation Proposal Accepted is 10 Percent Inspiration and 90 Percent Perspiration.*

SAMPLE

CONTENTS

BIBLIOGRAPHY

Aiken, J., & Cox, W. Vocational checklist. Unpublished test, 1970 (a).

Ary, D., Jacobs, L. & Razavieh, A. *Introduction to research in education.* New York: Holt, Rinehart & Winston, 1972.

Babbie, E. R. *Survey research methods.* Belmont, CA: Wadsworth Publishing Co., Inc., 1973.

Beatty, G. J. & Gardner, D. C. Goal setting and resume writing as a locus of control change technique with college women. *College Student Journal,* 1979, *13* (4).

Best, J. *Research in education.* Englewood Cliffs, NJ: Prentice-Hall, 1970.

Best, J. *Research in education.* Englewood Cliffs, NJ: Prentice-Hall, 1977.

Bigelow, E. Locus of control, career maturity and economic understanding. *Career Education Quarterly,* Winter, 1980.

Bohn, M. J., Jr. Vocational maturity and personality. *Vocational Guidance Quarterly,* 1966, *15,* (2), 123-125.

Campbell, D. T. & Stanley, J. C. *Experimental and quasi-experimental designs for research.* Chicago: Rand McNally, 1963.

Cowan, G. J. *The effects of teaching goal-setting procedures on the career maturity and classroom performance of business college women differing in locus in control.* Doctoral dissertation, Boston University, 1979.

Crites, J. O. *Administration and use manual for the Career Maturity Inventory.* Monterey, CA: CTB/McGraw-Hill, 1973.

Crites, J. O. *Career Maturity Inventory.* Monterey, CA: CTB/McGraw-Hill, 1973.

Crites, J. O. *Theory and research handbook for the Career Maturity Inventory.* Monterey, CA: CTB/McGraw-Hill, 1973.

Crites, J. O. A comprehensive model of career development in early adulthood. *Journal of Vocational Behavior,* 1976, *9,* 105-118.

Curry, J. *The effects of life planning instruction and career counseling on locus of control orientation and career maturity scores of university compensatory education students.* Doctoral dissertation, Boston University, 1980.

Dewey, B. *Factors affecting initial employment in special education.* Doctoral dissertation, Boston University, 1979.

Dipboye, R. L., Fromkin, H. L., & Wiback, K. Relative importance of applicant sex, attractiveness, and scholastic standing in evaluation of job applicant resumes. *Journal of Applied Psychology,* 1975, *60* (1), 39-43.

Dua, P. S. Comparison of the effects of behaviorally oriented action and psychotherapy reeducation on introversion-extraversion, emotionality, and internal-external control. *Journal of Counseling Psychology,* 1970, *17* (6), 567-572.

Felton, G. S. & Biggs, B. E. Teaching internalization behavior to collegiate low achievers in group psychotherapy. *Psychotherapy: Theory, Research and Practice,* 1972, *9* (3), 281-283.

Felton, G. S. & Biggs, B. E. Psychotherapy and responsibility: Teaching internalization behavior to black low achievers through group therapy. *Small Group Behavior,* 1973, *4* (2), 147-155.

Felton, G. S. & Davidson, H. R. Group counseling can work in the classroom. *Academic Therapy,* 1973, *8* (4), 461-468.

Gable, R. K. Perceptions of personal control and conformity of vocational choice as correlates of vocational development. ERIC Document No. ED 082 086. American Personnel and Guidance Association paper, 1973.

Galfo, A. J. & Miller, E. *Interpreting educational research.* Dubuque, Iowa: Wm. C. Brown Company Publishers, 1970.

Gardner, D. C. *Goal setting, locus of control, and work performance of mentally retarded adults.* Unpublished doctoral dissertation, Boston University, 1974 (b).

Gardner, D. C. & Beatty, G. J. Locus of control change techniques: Important variables in work training. *Education,* 100 (3), Spring, 1980, 237-242.

Gardner, D. C. & Gardner, P. L. Goal-setting and learning in the high school resource room. *Adolescence,* Fall, 1978, *13* (51), 489-493.

Gardner, D. C. & Gardner, P. L. Locus of control as related to learning effectiveness. *Reading Improvement,* 1974, *11* (2), 41-42.

Gardner, D. C. & Warren, S. *Careers and disabilities: A career education approach.* Stamford, Conn: Greylock Publishers, 1978 (a).

Gardner, D. C. & Warren, S. *Different situations inventory.* Copyright, 1978 (b).

Ginzberg, E., Ginsburg, S. W., Axelrad, S., & Herma, J. L. *Occupational choice.* NY: Columbia University, University Press, 1951.

Grinker, R. R., Sr. & Spiegel, J. P. *Men under stress.* Philadelphia: Blakiston, 1945.

Grossman, B. J. *Effects of decision-making skill instruction on locus of control, career choice competency and occupational information-seeking behavior.* Doctoral dissertation, Boston University, 1979.

Guilford, J. P. *Fundamental statistics in psychology and education.* NY: McGraw-Hill, 1965.

Guilford, J. & Fruchter, B. *Fundamental statistics in psychology and education.* New York: McGraw-Hill, 1978.

Hakel, M. D. & Mannel, C. H. If at first you don't succeed. *Journal of College Placement,* 1969, *29* (2), 65-70.

Hoyt, K. B. *Career education: contributions to an evolving concept.* Salt Lake

City: Olympus Publishing Co., 1975.

Ifenwanta, S. S. *Locus of control, career maturity, and perceived needs for lifelong education of Nigerian students in the United States.* Doctoral dissertation, Boston University. 1978.

Issac, S. & Michael, W. *Handbook in research and evaluation.* San Diego: Edits Publishers, 1971.

Isaac, S. *Handbook in research and evaluation.* San Diego: Edits Publishers, 1977.

James, W. H. Internal vs. external control of reinforcement as a basic variable in learning theory. Doctoral Dissertation, Ohio State University, 1957.

Kerlinger, F. N. *Foundations of behavioral research* (Second edition). New York: Holt, Rinehart, and Winston, 1964.

Kerlinger, F. & Pedhazur, E. *Multiple regression in behavioral research.* New York: Holt, Rinehart and Winston, 1973.

Kimmel, H. D. *Experimental principles and design in psychology.* New York: Ronald Press Co., 1970.

Kleinbaum, D. & Kupper, L. *Applied regression analysis and other multivariable methods.* North Scituate, MA: Duxbury Press, 1978.

Kurtz, M. A. *The effects of goal setting and anxiety on accuracy of production typing task performance.* Doctoral dissertation, Boston University, 1978.

MacDonald, A. P., Jr. Internal-external locus of control: A promising rehabilitation variable. *Journal of Counseling Psychology,* 1971, *18* (2), 111-116.

MacDonald, A. P. Jr. Internal-external locus of control change-technics. *Rehabilitation Literature,* 1972, *33* (2), 44-47 (a).

MacDonald, A. P., Jr. *Internal-external locus of control: A partial bibliography.* Morgantown: West Virginia University, 1972 (b).

MacDonald, A. P., Jr. Internal-external locus of control: A partial bibliography, part II. *Catalog of Selected Documents in Psychology,* 1972, *2* (2) (c).

Majumder, R. K., Greever, K. B., Holt, P. R. & Friedland, B. U. Counseling techniques tested: Field study shows effective internal/external counseling. *Journal of Rehabilitation,* 1973, *39* (5), 19-22.

Moreland, H. W. *Goal setting, anxiety and learning disabled children.* Doctoral dissertation, Boston University, 1977.

Moser, C. A. *Survey methods in social investigation.* London: Heinemann, 1961.

Nixon, G. F., Jr. The relationship between anxiety-trait and anxiety-state with the approach of final examinations. (Doctoral dissertation, East Texas University, 1969) *Dissertation Abstracts International,* 1969, *30,* 5296A. (University Microfilms No. 70-11, 298.)

Nunnally, J. *Psychometric theory.* New York: McGraw-Hill, 1978.

O'Neil, H. F., Jr., Hansen, D. N. & Spielberger, C. D. *The effects of state and trait anxiety on computer-assisted learning.* Unpublished paper, 1969.

O'Neil, H. F., Jr., Spielberger, C. D. & Hansen, D. N. Effects of state anxiety and task difficulty on computer-assisted learning. *Journal of Educational Psychology*. 1969, *60* (5), 343-350.

Parten, M. *Surveys, polls, and samples: practical procedures.* New York: Cooper Square Publishers, 1966.

Payne, S. L. *The art of asking questions.* Princeton, NJ: Princeton University Press, 1951.

Phares, E. J. *Locus of control in personality.* Morristown, NJ: General Learning Press, 1976.

Reimanis, G. The effects of locus of reinforcement control modification procedures in early graders and college students. *Journal of Educational Research,* 1974, *68,* 124-127.

Roscoe, J. *Fundamental research statistics.* New York: Holt, Rinehart, and Winston, 1969.

Rotter, J. B. *Social learning and clinical psychology.* Englewood Cliffs, NJ: Prentice-Hall, 1954.

Rotter, J. B. Some implications of a social learning theory for the prediction of goal-directed behavior from testing procedures. *Psychological Review,* 1960, *67,* (5), 301-316.

Rotter, J. B. Generalized expectancies for internal vs. external control of reinforcement. *Psychological Monographs,* 1966, *80,* (1).

Rotter, J. B., Chance, J. E., & Phares, E. J. *Application of social learning theory of personality.* New York: Holt, Rinehart, and Winston, 1972.

Rotter, J. B. Some problems and misconceptions related to the construct of internal vs. external control of reinforcement. *Journal of Consulting and Clinical Psychology,* 1975, *43* (1), 56-67.

Siegel, S. *Nonparametric statistics for the behavioral sciences.* New York: McGraw-Hill, 1956.

Spielberger, C. D. (Ed.). *Anxiety and behavior.* New York: Academic Press, 1966.

Spielberger, C. D. (Ed.). Anxiety: *Current trends in theory and research.* New York: Academic Press, 1972.

Spielberger, C. D. (Ed.). The effects of manifest anxiety on the academic achievement of college students. *Mental Hygiene,* 1962, *46,* 420-426.

Spielberger, C. D., Gorsuch, R. L., & Lushene, R. E. *STAI Manual.* Palo Alto, CA: Consulting Psychologists Press, Inc., 1970.

Super, D. E. A theory of vocational development. *American Psychologist,* 1953, *8* (4), 185-190.

Super, D. E. *Career education and the meaning of work.* Monographs on Career Education, U. S. Department of Health, Education and Welfare, June, 1976.

Teacher supply and demand in public schools 1974/1975/1976 with population trends and their implication for schools 1976-1977. *A National Education Association Publication.* Washington, D.C.: National Education Association, 1977.

Thomas, H. B. The effects of sex, occupational choice, and career development responsibility on the career maturity of ninth-grade students. ERIC Document No. ED 092 819. American Educational Research Association paper, 1974 (a).

Thomas, H. B. A measure of career development responsibility. ERIC Document No. ED 093 935. National Council on Measurement in Education paper, 1974 (b).

Tiedeman, D. V. Decisions and vocational development: A paradigm and its implications. *Personnel and Guidance Journal,* 1961, *40,* 15-21.

vonEsch, P. *An inquiry into the effects of a syncretic application of locus of control change techniques to a manpower training program for the economically disadvantaged.* Doctoral dissertation, Boston University, 1978.

Webb, E., Campbell, D., Schwartz, R. & Sechrest, L. *Unobtrusive measures: Nonreactive research in the social sciences.* Chicago: Rand McNally, 1966.

Weiss, C. *Evaluation research.* Englewood Cliffs, NJ: Prentice-Hall, 1972.

Wilton, T. L. *Sex differences in career development: Social desirability as a cultural role mediator in analyzing locus of control and career maturity of middle school students.* Doctoral dissertation, Boston University, 1978.

INDEX

95